The European Insurance Industry

Antonella Cappiello

The European Insurance Industry

Regulation, Risk Management, and Internal Control

palgrave
macmillan

Antonella Cappiello
Department of Economics and Management
University of Pisa
Pisa, Italy

ISBN 978-3-030-43141-9 ISBN 978-3-030-43142-6 (eBook)
https://doi.org/10.1007/978-3-030-43142-6

This Palgrave Macmillan imprint is published by the registered company Springer Nature Switzerland AG
The registered company address is: Gewerbestrasse 11, 6330 Cham, Switzerland

Contents

List of Tables

Chapter 6

CHAPTER 1

Introduction

Abstract This chapter introduces the aim of the book and sets its theoretical framework by providing a guideline for the topics included in each chapter.

Keywords European insurance industry · Solvency II Directive · Insurance regulation and supervision · Enterprise risk management · Insurance risk management · Risk assessment · Internal control

The continuously evolving complexity of the risk system accentuates the uncertain context in which the modern enterprise must operate. In this context, the insurance undertaking, which institutionally assumes risks transferred from other economies as its core business, is itself exposed to the risk that notoriously pervades all companies. Therefore, over time the management team must define the level of uncertainty that the undertaking can accept, i.e. the level of vulnerability compatible with the value creation objectives.

Though risk governance is a distinctive trait and an essential and fundamental component of business management by definition, the growth of success of the risk culture within insurance management companies seems to be a rather new conquest, primarily deriving from the significant changes in the insurance sector in recent years.

In the European context, the Directive 2009/138/EC, also known as Solvency II, and which came into force on 1 January 2016, imposed a

A. Cappiello, *The European Insurance Industry*,
https://doi.org/10.1007/978-3-030-43142-6_1

structured and global paradigm to protect company solvency according to a risk-based approach, one which places at the centre of the supervisor, undertakings and market's attention, the quantity and quality of risk that all undertakings assume with their financial resource investment decisions and commitment towards insured parties.

From a systematic perspective, the Solvency II supervisory framework is structured across three pillars. The first pillar sets out the quantitative solvency requirements, which, in a risk-based overview, in addition to the capital requirements considers the correct assessment of all obligations towards policyholders, the diversification of investments and their coherence with the liabilities and risk appetite defined by senior management, the profitability and sustainability of products offered over time and the capability to mitigate technical and financial risks.

Nevertheless, we know that the simple quantitative measures are not always sufficient to identify and appropriately define all risks to which a company is exposed. Solvency II does not simply require that insurance companies have appropriate capital requirements to tackle the various company risks, it also encourages them to develop a genuine corporate risk culture in order to protect shareholders, lenders and stakeholders in general. The Board of Directors and the senior management team are the first to be called upon to meet high standards of ethics and integrity, so as to spread said culture to all company levels.

Consequently, within the second pillar the Solvency II Directive confirms the central role of control activities and the functions assigned to overseeing the internal controls system as fundamental elements of an effective governance system intended to provide for a sound and prudent management of the business.

The integrated management of the various company risks must acknowledge, now more than ever, the preparation of adequate internal control systems to identify and cushion the risk potentially undermining tangible value creation in a business area such as insurance, which has unique operating profiles.

The internal controls system, also according to the ratio of supervisory regulations, must be understood as all the regulations, procedures and organisational structures used to ensure the undertaking's correct functioning and good performance in accordance with the pre-established objectives. It must then be used to pursue, with a good level of security: the efficiency and effectiveness of company processes; a valid risk control;

the integrity and reliability of the accounting and management information; the monitoring of the undertaking's assets; and the compliance of the undertaking's activities with law and regulations.

An effective control system must guarantee a close interconnection with all other variables present within the company system such as organisational, individual, technical and social variables. This system must present a clear distribution and appropriate segregation of responsibilities, in addition to making it possible to transmit information effectively. The Solvency II's second pillar envisages a corporate governance system based on a system of internal controls and risk management structured across the following four functions—all pertaining to the end responsibility of the company Board: risk management, compliance, internal audit and actuarial function, which must bolster the "three lines of defence" structure.

Current trends in the insurance and financial sector therefore impose on undertakings the need to develop increasingly sophisticated business control mechanisms that are capable of monitoring and constantly managing the growing operational complexity and correlated risk profiles.

Following the financial crisis, the issue of risk governance in the financial sector rose to prominence. Risk governance may be defined as the framework of rules, relationships, systems and processes within organisations with regard to the management and control of risk. This involves a stronger risk oversight according to an enterprise-wide risk management approach. Though insurance companies were affected to a lesser extent by the financial crisis than banks, and their core business—risk underwriting—did not feel its effects, it has nevertheless been demonstrated that insurance companies with a stronger risk governance structure might be able to better control their shortfall risk.

Nevertheless, it is necessary to mention that risk governance must not only be considered a defensive activity. During non-crisis periods, the purpose of risk governance is not to reduce risk per se, but to support appropriate risk-taking and increase the probability that a firm might achieve its business objectives.

In this respect, the ever more central role of the risk management function is revealed, now seen as a concrete governance tool in support of the administrative body. Diligent risk management, no longer only considered as a burden to bear, but recognised as a possible success factor, may allow for a tangible increase in efficiency in company resource allocation, so as to guarantee an improvement of those company performances and a concrete competitive advantage.

The development of the risk culture, i.e. a system of shared values and common regulations created in the undertaking in order to protect it from the risks to which it is exposed, is therefore fundamental for correct risk management activities, provided that said culture makes it possible to acquire awareness of the risks, communicate the information obtained during their assessment and contribute to their management in an effective and efficient way.

No longer informally managed, relationships evolve by necessity towards an ever greater integration in terms of models, methodologies and tools in order to adequately capture all types of risk, including those not currently reported or even for which the related quantitative models have not been developed.

It is essential to bolster and organise an enormous amount of technical and financial abilities within the risk management function, independently of the operating functions, in order to still guarantee autonomous and clear reporting in relation to the risks considered.

A fair and appropriate identification and assessment of risk requires the continuous collection, by the undertaking itself, of information regarding the internal, external, existing and prospective risks it may incur during its activities, involving all operating processes and functional areas.

The demand for integrated databases that are easy to consult and contain the most complete and processable information undoubtedly represents the starting point for a *risk sensitive approach* when creating company policies and defining supervisory requirements from a Solvency II perspective.

Adopting an integrated risk management system, with consolidating strength with respect to considering the risks to which the company is exposed, maybe very complex; this complexity must not, however, serve as a deterrent when undertaking the overall project.

The book is divided into six chapters including the Introduction.

Chapter 2 highlights the peculiarity of features and risks that insurance undertakings have to face. Consequently, it focuses on the role of internal control systems, which become a key concern to cope with the complexity of insurance activity. The chapter ends by analysing the motivation and evolution of external regulation using a European and international vision

Chapter 3 focuses on the role and characteristics of a systemic approach to risk governance capable of tackling the growing complexity of the uncertainty in the financial markets, and within them, the activities of insurance intermediaries. In this context, the Enterprise Risk Management (ERM) process enables firms to approach risks in an enterprise-wide, consolidated, structured, dynamic and continuous manner from a long-term perspective. The chapter concludes by focusing on an integrated approach to the classification, assessment, management and control of the various risks faced by the insurance sector: not only underwriting and reserve risk—typical of the insurance sector—but also market, credit, liquidity, operational and compliance risk.

Chapter 4 analyses the regulatory principles of the second pillar of Solvency II, which is constituted by provisions pertaining to corporate governance, risk management and the internal control system and, secondly, by the regulation of supervisory activities, instruments and powers. In particular, the chapter focuses on the key four functions of the risk governance system: risk management, compliance, actuarial and audit function, which bolster the "three lines of defence" structure.

Chapter 5 highlights current trends in the insurance and financial sector and analyses how internal controls of undertakings have to be adapted to better cope with the evolving scenario, where insurance activities become ever riskier and more complex. Furthermore, the chapter focuses on the impact of these potential changes on external regulation and on the needed revision of the existing regulatory regime.

Chapter 6 proposes an assessment model in order to enable the internal audit function to express a synthetic opinion about the company's internal control system on an annual basis. The model is constructed starting from the risk types defined by the company organisational model, identified within the entity level risks—which affect the overall company structure—and within the process level risks, which affect individual company processes and are influenced by the first ones.

CHAPTER 2

Risks and Control of Insurance Undertakings

Abstract Insurance companies are exposed to some risks that can be controlled as well as to some which are difficult to foresee. They are exposed not only to internal risks, but also to external ones. The length of some insurance contracts, which may run for many years, may compound these risks. The chapter highlights the peculiarity of features and of risks (life and non-life insurance) that the insurance undertakings have to face. Consequently, it focuses on the role of internal control systems, which become a key concern to cope with the complexity of insurance activity. The chapter ends by analysing the motivation and evolution of external supervision and regulation using a European and international vision.

Keywords Insurance intermediation · Insurance risks · Internal control · External supervision and regulation · Solvency II · USA solvency regime

1 Introduction

Insurance companies have always performed a fundamental role within the financial and economic system in relation to the essential element of their activity, including at social level, which can be identified in the ability to protect companies and families from unknown and unpredictable events and situations through the assumption and management of their related risks.

A. Cappiello, *The European Insurance Industry*,
https://doi.org/10.1007/978-3-030-43142-6_2

The function of insurance is to provide protection against events through the pooling of individual risks. Insurance companies combine the risks of various people in a pool, and can spread the risks over this (large) group of insured (De Finetti and Emanuelli 1967; Cassandro 1975; Borch et al. 1990; De Haan et al. 2015).

Like banks, insurance companies carry out a financial intermediation, using the premiums collected from underwriting activity to invest them in various assets used to meet the obligations assumed towards the policyholders (Mishkin and Eakins 2018; Hull 2018; Outreville 1998).

Insurance is usually classified as life insurance and nonlife insurance (sometimes also called property-casualty insurance), with health insurance often being considered to be a separate category.

Life insurance contract protects against premature death, and typically lasts a long time. While it is difficult to predict the death of an individual, death rates for large populations are fairly stable and therefore easier to predict.

A property-casualty insurance contract typically lasts one year (although it may be renewed) and provides compensation for losses from accidents, fire, theft and so on. The risk dynamic of non-life insurance are more diverse than those of life insurance. Relatedly small accidents are fairly predictable and can easily be pooled by an insurance company. On the other hand, larger accidents or catastrophes are low-probability but high-impact events. The risk related to these events is too great for a single insurance company and therefore is divided between different insurance and reinsurance companies (Hull 2018; Santoboni 2017).

2 Distinctive Features and Risks of Insurance Undertakings

The financial intermediary nature is assigned to insurers by the doctrinal approaches that justify their creation and existence in the imperfect context of the financial markets, and insurance market in particular, which are characterised by asymmetrical information essentially attributable to ***adverse selection*** and ***moral hazard behaviours*** (Arnott and Stiglitz 1991; Finkelstein et al. 2015).

Under the assumption of full information, complete insurance is possible at actuarially fair premium rates. However complete coverage is not always available in insurance markets due to asymmetric information. In this regard, two key risks in insurance are moral hazard and adverse selection. Insurance companies take steps to reduce these two types of risk, but they cannot eliminate them altogether (Handel 2013).

Moral hazard is the risk that the behaviour of an individual or corporation with an insurance contract will be different from the behaviour without the insurance contract. This different behaviour increases the risks and the expected payouts of the insurance company (Kesternich and Schumacher 2014). Complete coverage may not be attainable under moral hazard, due to the trade-off between the goal of efficient risk-sharing, which is met by allocating the risk to the insurer, and the goal of efficient incentives, which requires leaving the consequences of decision about care with the decision-maker, i.e. the insured.

On the other hand, adverse selection arises when an insurance company cannot distinguish between good and bad risks. It offers the same price to everyone and inadvertently attracts more of the bad risks (Rothschild and Stiglitz 1976). To lessen the impact of adverse selection, an insurance company tries to find out as much as possible about the policyholder before committing itself (Boadway et al. 2014; Dionne et al. 2012).

When people take out insurance policies to satisfy mostly security needs, they transfer savings shares to the insurance companies, which in turn sell those resources to the deficit units through investment in real and financial assets, thereby stimulating the development of economic activity (Arrow 1970).

The financial resources deriving from underwriting activity, at least as long as the probability of risk occurrence remains, must be appropriately invested in order to guarantee the undertaking's capacity to systematically comply with compensation obligations on the one hand, and, on the other, to produce income flows that allow for a reduction of insurance service prices, the mitigation of technical cost weighting, the improvement of profits and the strengthening of the undertaking's capital structure. This gives the strict correlation and mutual influence between insurance function and financial function.

Even if insurers invest resources collected from the public, it proves beneficial to underline how, in any case, it is a form of atypical intermediation if referring to other financial system intermediaries, compared to which insurers present keenly different characteristics (Paci 1979).

Irrespective of the impossibility to attribute monetary function to the insurance liabilities, hence the impossibility to include insurance undertakings among bank intermediaries (Bianchi 1975), we must note the character of uncertainty that intrinsically distinguishes the liabilities—in this case, the technical provisions—of insurance undertakings. Indeed, these are characterised by *contingent liabilities*, i.e. liabilities subject to the occurrence of a given event. The uncertainty, which is more pronounced in the case of non-life insurance companies, is nevertheless present in the life insurance. Due to this, though the obligation towards all policyholders is certain, the time frame remains uncertain.

The financial intermediation function, variously defined and justified in its founding moment by the various doctrinal approaches, therefore presents, within the insurance sector, entirely unique connotations attributable to the intrinsic characteristics of the production processes. A dual process of transformation and transfer can be identified with reference to both raw materials subject to insurance production, i.e. "risk" and "money".

The originality of insurance intermediation indeed lies in the coincidence between the technical management of risks and the monetary dimension of insurance contracts.

The complexity of insurance management in relation to actuarial and financial risk governance is certainly increased by the two different intermediation profiles—risk assumption and management on the one hand, formation of technical provisions and investment of corresponding resources on the other—though attributable to units in the common financial matrix.

Specifically, the main risk types for an insurer are underwriting risk, market risk, liquidity risk, credit risk and operational risk.

The first type of risk is *underwriting risk*. Insurers make provisions for future claims. An unforeseen increase in the size and frequency of claims may mean that the policy reserves are not sufficient to meet the claims of policyholders. Although the calculations of actuaries are usually fairly conservative, there is always the chance that payouts much higher than anticipated will be required.

Insurance companies also face *market risk*, concerned with the performance of their investments, many of those are in corporate bonds. If defaults on corporate bonds are above average, the profitability of the insurance company will suffer. It is important that an insurance company's bond portfolio be diversified by business sector and geographical region.

An insurance company also needs to monitor the *liquidity risks* associated with its investments. Illiquid bonds (e.g. those the insurance company might buy in a private placement) tend to provide higher yields than bonds that are publicly owned and actively traded. However, they cannot be as readily converted into cash to meet unexpectedly high claims.

Insurance companies enter into transactions with issuers of financial instruments, banks and reinsurance companies. This exposes them to *credit risk*. Like banks, insurance companies are also exposed to *operational risks* arising from loss from inadequate internal processes, people or systems, or from external events (see Chapter 3).

Despite some similarities between banking and insurance intermediaries, the impact of the various types of risk differs across these two financial intermediaries, deriving from the core business of both. Since the main business of banks is granting loans, credit risk is the most important risk driver in banking, followed by market and asset and liability (ALM) risk. ALM risk is related to the duration of long-term investments, which are related to the collection of short-term deposits.

In relation to the distinction between life and non-life insurance, we can state that underwriting risk is the main risk driver for P&C insurers. In life insurance, the main risk is market risk related to the large asset portfolio invested with long-term maturities. The second risk in life insurance is ALM risk, that is the opposite of banking ALM risk. Indeed, while among banking sector ALM risk is caused by long-term assets founded by short-term deposits, life insurers typically invest the premiums on their long-term policies in shorter-lived assets.

3 The Role of Internal Control

The changes to the international economic scenario have ensured that the risk level that a firm is willing to accept in order to create value constitutes one of the most crucial challenges the management team must face. From this perspective, internal control has become a key concern, as insurance activities become ever riskier and more complex.

The modern conception of controls is based around the notion of corporate risks, their identification, assessment and monitoring; for this reason, legislation and codes of conduct also refer to the internal control and risk management system as a unitary system where risk represents the underlying theme.

From the insurance sector point of view, internal control should be seen as an opportunity for the undertaking to improve their performance, both from an internal and an external perspective.

Internally, good internal control systems lead to improved recognition, assumption and prevention of risks, which is of prime importance in a sector with the particularities of insurance, which is about finding business opportunities in risks. Also, competitiveness will be fostered by appropriate controls not only in the short but also in the long term. Finally, it will help reduce the impact of unexpected events, or even to avoid them altogether, for example by means of good early warnings or scenario testing (Ozigbo and Orife 2011; Kasturi 2006).

Externally, appropriate internal control systems will have a positive impact on policyholders—meaning better results for the undertaking, supervisors and shareholders—meaning higher confidence and thus higher share value of the entity.

Internal control systems should help entities to improve performance both in favourable and unfavourable situations and conditions; execute the business plan; exploit business opportunities; mitigate adverse effects of both internal and external effects, creating an added value for the company (Olajide 2013).

It follows that the internal control should strengthen the internal operating environment of the company, thereby increasing its capability to deal with external (and internal) events and uncover possible flaws and deficiencies in processes and structures.

Taking into account that the Board and management are responsible for establishing and maintaining an appropriate system of internal control, internal controls will be affected by the way the undertaking is managed, and therefore by corporate governance. There is a link between internal control and the way an entity is managed, whether in a positive or a negative way, thus internal control should be seen as a core part of corporate governance. The Sharma Report of the European Commission in 2002, and later the European Insurance and Occupational Pensions Authority (EIOPA) in 2018 found that poor management was a key underlying factor in the failure or near failure of many European insurance companies (European Commission 2002; EIOPA 2018).

Internal control is about understanding and controlling risk, as well as acting as a monitoring function. The primary purpose of internal control is to continuously evaluate whether a firm is meeting its objectives and to ensure that the board, managers and employees are all working to ensure the success of these strategies while keeping the level of risk at an acceptable level. In so doing a sound system of internal control should be able to reduce (but rarely eliminate) poor judgement in decision-making; human error; the deliberate failure to follow control processes by employees and managers; and the impact of unexpected events.

Internal control is carried out by the Board, management and all personnel: everyone in the undertaking has an internal control responsibility appropriate to their role in the undertaking, and the board and management will be responsible for the establishment, maintenance and improvement of the internal control systems of the entity. In addition, internal control affects all personnel's work, decisions or assumptions, in their daily work and in the long term as well.

The most widely recognised internal controls framework was developed in 1992 by the Committee of Sponsoring Organizations of the Treadway Commission (CoSO). While it has been updated since then (CoSO 1992, 2013), the fundamentals have not changed.

CoSO defines internal control as "…a process, effected by an entity's board of directors, management, and other personnel, designed to provide reasonable assurance regarding the achievement of objectives relating to operations, reporting and compliance" (CoSO 1992).

Internal Control systems are intended to help achieving certain goals and objectives, including the following:

- Operational objective (effectiveness and efficiency of operations);
- Information objective (reliability of financial and non-financial information);
- Control objective (an adequate control of risks);
- Management objective (a prudent approach to business);
- Compliance objective (compliance with laws and regulations, and internal policies and procedures).

The systemic vision of the CoSO framework defines five integrated components—control environment, risk assessment, control activities, information and communication and monitoring of internal control activities—across the three categories of objectives: operational objectives, reporting objectives and compliance objectives. To achieve its overall purpose, internal control is dependent on how effective each of its elements functions and how well they are coordinated and integrated with each other (Gupta 2006).

Control environment: determines the climate in which the various parties perform their activities and their own control functions, and represents the basis for all other components of the system. For this reason, it forms the substrate of the other elements, significantly impacting the structuring of activities, setting of objectives and assessment of risks.

In order to have adequate internal control systems, insurance undertakings should have an organisational culture at all levels of the company that is conscious and aware of the importance of internal control. It is the responsibility of the Board of Directors (the Board) and management to emphasise the importance of internal control through their actions and words. This includes the ethical values that the company displays in their business dealings, both inside and outside the organisation.

Risk assessment: in establishing and maintaining an effective system of internal control an insurance undertaking should regularly assess both the internal and external risks that it faces. Assessment should include the identification and analysis (using quantitative and/or qualitative tools) of all the significant risks that an insurance company is exposed to, and act accordingly (D'Onza 2008).

Control activities: include all policies and procedures that must be developed and applied to ensure that management directives are carried out and to reduce the risk of not meeting the company objectives. An adequate internal control system requires the implementation of effective and efficient control activities at all levels of the entity. They should be implemented by the management in line with the goals and strategies set up by the Board, and should involve all personnel. As an integrated part of daily business, these activities should be reviewed and recorded on an ongoing basis. Control activities should be linked to the risk assessment processes, as long as they tackle those risks previously identified and analysed by the insurance undertaking. They should address efficiently the process of defining adequate limits for exposure to risk as well as policies and procedures aiming to adjust business activities to the strategic decisions the risk profile.

Information and communication: insurance undertakings should have reliable information at all levels within their organisation, in order to define, achieve and review the objectives settled by the Board, through effective decision-making processes. Internal control systems should ensure the effectiveness of communication procedures. Such communication should be internal as well as external, and may include both formal and informal paths.

Insurance undertakings should have both financial and non-financial information relating to the past and current situation of the entity, obtained both on internal and on external bases. The same rule of thumb should apply to operational data, for example data on compliance with external regulations and internal procedures.

Monitoring: Insurance undertakings should implement appropriate monitoring systems for their internal controls' efficiency and effectiveness. Monitoring should be carried out on an ongoing basis, complemented with separate evaluations.

4 The Role of External Supervision and Regulation

The economic and social impact of the insurance industry is, notoriously, of such an extent that it leads to the common belief that a public prudential supervisory system is necessary.

While operating, insurance companies find themselves exposed to a series of risks that endanger their capacity to uphold the obligations assumed towards policyholders. This issue, which introduces the concept of solvency, has taken on great importance not only for the parties that manage the entirety of the insurance sector, but also for the national and international supervisory authorities, whose end goal is to guarantee the stability of the whole economic system (Spencer 2000; Kessler 2008).

Insurance company insolvency may have disproportionately high costs for the customer, and even for society as a whole, compared to insolvency in other industries.

This is partly because policyholders buy insurance to protect themselves against a particular loss, so when the loss occurs and the insurance company becomes insolvent and unable to pay the claim, it is possible that the policyholder's very economic existence is jeopardised. The insolvency of an insurance company can also affect the economic existence of a third party, for example, in the case of liability insurance.

Imperfect information on the solvency status of insurance companies, combined with the severe consequences of insurance company failures, make regulation of the insurance industry, with the aim of decreasing the risk of insolvency, of public interest (Holzmuller 2009).

However, regulation comes at a cost. Although a well-designed regulatory framework can reduce the risk of insurer insolvency, it can also distort the decisions of financially sound insurers. These distortions create market inefficiencies, leading to an eventually even lower safety level and higher premium prices. Also, ineffective regulatory frameworks can give insurance companies, the regulator and policyholders a false sense of security.

Capital regulation has changed dramatically; the former volume-driven capital requirements have, for the most part, been replaced by risk-sensitive capital requirements. Both European and national legislators have undertaken to draft new regulations on insurance supervision that respond to the changes in the insurance and capital markets, including, for example, the convergence of the banking and insurance sectors, and the increasing complexity and interdependence of insurer assets and liabilities (Van Rossum 2005).

Recent decades have seen a process of convergence within the financial industry along three dimensions: between financial institutions and capital markets; among different types of financial institutions; and among different national jurisdictions.

These powerful forces of convergence have been mirrored in developments in risk management and in the prudential frameworks adopted by national authorities.

With risk management evolving from a side constraint on financial activity to a core function underpinning that activity, the similarities between the risks faced by different institutions have become increasingly apparent.

Mentioned briefly, the above has gone hand in hand with efforts to move towards a more integrated firm-wide approach to risk management. Across business lines, this means managing the same risk in the same way regardless of its location in an enterprise. Across different types of risk, it means developing a common metric for the aggregation of risks and for the calibration of economic capital. Clearly, even cutting-edge enterprises are a long way from achieving either objective.

Likewise, prudential frameworks have been converging along different dimensions. Across national jurisdictions, it has become increasingly difficult to pursue country-specific solutions. International cooperation through the establishment of common standards, initially spearheaded in banking by the Basel Committee, has subsequently encompassed other regulatory groupings too, first securities regulators and then insurance supervisors (Insurance Europe 2014; Krischanitz 2013). Across functional lines, the differences in approach have narrowed. For instance, capital adequacy, supervisory review of risk management processes, and enhanced public disclosures are all core elements of the prudential frameworks for both banking and insurance. The trend towards convergence has been strengthened by the establishment of "integrated supervisors" in a number of countries.

4.1 Evolutionary Profiles of the Solvency Regime in the European Context

On a supranational scale, the European Union has intervened over time on several occasions with provisions for progressive regulatory standardisation. The first regulation experiments on insurance company solvency profiles date back to the beginning of the 1970s, with Directives 73/239/EEC and 79/267/EEC.

Nearly twenty years after these measures, the "third-generation" Insurance Directives stepped up to the plate with the introduction of a single licence for insurers, in line with the Community principles of home country control and mutual recognition (Dir. 92/49/EEC and Dir. 92/96/EEC).

These directives made no change to the prudential regulation regarding capital requirements (solvency margin), dating back to the first life insurance and non-life insurance directives; however, here began the aim to standardise provisions on the matter.

The related trend was completed with EU Directives nos. 12 and 13 of 2002 governing the supervisory regime—known as Solvency I—for the solvency margin of insurance companies, on life insurance and non-life insurance, respectively.

The legislation strengthened supervision by imposing the obligation to continuously maintain the solvency capital requirements (SCRs), and not only at the date of preparation of the financial statements, and extended the supervisory authorities' power of intervention.

The regulations of the Solvency I regime left the solvency margin calculation methods essentially unchanged. In practice the solvency margin was calculated, within the life insurance, as a percentage of the technical provisions, and in the non-life insurance as a percentage of the annual premiums or average cost of the claims.

The positive valuation regarding the regulatory infrastructure's unquestionable simplicity was starkly contrasted by certain shortcomings and limitations of the capital requirement calculation mechanism.

One of the main critical elements substantially concerned the application of near unique rates to the technical parameters, which were occasionally inadequate at approximating portfolio risks.

The results of these calculations merely form an approximate parameter of the risk, given that this may change, even consistently, in relation to the variable operating conditions and the context of reference (Paci 2004; Eling et al. 2007).

These practices inevitably penalised larger firms, since we know that growth in the risk portfolio volume is not accompanied by a directly proportional increase in the number of claims.

This is true in both the non-life insurance, where as the number of insured units increases the number of claims tends to stabilise more than might occur in a smaller portfolio, and in the life insurance, where as the volume of premiums and the number of policyholders grow, the gap between demographic bases adopted in the pricing and effective mortality generally decreases. Therefore, it would be preferable to envisage a decreasing incidence of the solvency margin as the volume of at-risk capital increases.

In addition, Solvency I did not take into account the qualitative profiles of the insurance portfolio or the loans made to hedge it. For example, in order to determine the solvency requirement in the non-life insurance, the composition of the liabilities portfolio was not assessed whatsoever, even if some branches at higher risk of an excessive claims rate would require a greater level of capitalisation compared to others.

The exclusive focus on technical items, with no reference to the composition of the assets portfolio and the related financial risks, may cause a possible misalignment in assets/liabilities management. As a matter of fact, it was possible that companies with the same liabilities risk profile, but with liabilities at different levels of risk, had to meet the same capital requirements.

The foregoing places emphasis on how the Solvency I calculation system was not able to report the individual risk profiles appropriately, but rather only identified one level of capital requirement as a supplementary and global guarantee of sound management.

Moreover, in other respects, the regulation in question leaves itself wide open to rather significant criticism. We make particular reference to the scarce connection, if any, with the prudential technical provisions regulation, the investments to cover them, the lack of attention paid to the benefits deriving from diversification and diverse forms of risk mitigation, and moreover, to how closely the solvency margin depends on the balance sheet values, which are inevitably influenced by the valuation criteria of the assets and liabilities.

It is apparent that meeting the capital requirements was not deemed a sufficient guarantee of solvency, unless this was accompanied by careful company policies and adequate risk control systems.

After all, many bankruptcies in the insurance sector are demonstrated not only to be related to capital shortfall, but rather to the more or less manifest non-observance of other requirements such as insufficient technical provisions, imprudent decisions regarding investments and inadequate pricing policies; this in joined by low-quality management (EIOPA 2018).

Lastly, we see that Solvency I outlined a fragmented patchwork regulation in the European area. Though the directives did indeed provide the minimum standardisation level for the Community, each country was nevertheless free to decide independently on the concrete solvency margin calculation methods, providing a somewhat inhomogeneous picture of the prudential supervisory structure. Some countries followed Solvency I rigorously; others opted for a risk-based regulation.

Not to mention the consequences created by the growing internationalisation of the insurance industry with the birth of more groups present in several countries, and obligated to meet the most diverse prudential regulations at a time when, with the European passport, their policies had free access in the continental market.

From here came the EU bodies' intention to undertake a wide-scale review of the prudential supervisory regime, intended to include all factors influencing the solvency conditions of insurance companies, calling upon those companies to perform a fairer global evaluation of business risk where capital requirements are only one of the reference parameters (European Commission 2007).

4.2 Genesis and Purposes of the Solvency II Regulation in Europe

Having undertaken the Solvency II project in 2001, in November 2003 the European Commission established a permanent committee tasked with writing a draft framework law. The intention, as outlined above, was to promote profound innovation in the prudential supervision regulations in the insurance sector and spread increasing convergence between international and intersectoral regulation, in order to guarantee a level playing field where all competitors might operate under equivalent regulatory conditions.

The process of transposing the Solvency II Directive into the legislation of the 28 Member States of the European Union has followed a long and complex path, which is still being completed. Important corrections to the original directive were introduced in 2014 in light of the bitter experience of the global crisis. Solvency II was amended by Directive 2014/51/EU (known as Omnibus II), which attributed more powers of control to the EIOPA. Finally, the Solvency II Directive, postponed several times, has been set for all Member States on 1 January 2016 (Doff 2016; Heisen et al. 2014).

The introduction of the Solvency II regulatory framework represented a significant change in the supervisory system—in the not-so-short term—for insurance undertakings. Solvency II framework is based on a dynamic risk-based approach, in order to achieve a quantitative and qualitative measure of the risks arising from the insurance business and to improve its performance and operating efficiency.

Experience has shown the clear responsibilities of moderate-quality management in establishing crises in insurance undertakings. This clearly denounces the basic issue posed by the Directive: acknowledging the insufficiency or inadequacy of only considering quantitative requirements with a view to crisis prevention. In turn, within this renewed dimension, it is clear that conscious management is the first defence for company solvency.

Comprehensive insight allows us to state that Solvency II adopts a global solvency approach which provides the supervisory authorities with the adequate tools and powers to assess the overall solvency of all types of insurance companies, based on a forward-looking and risk-oriented analysis.

From a systematic point of view, the regulatory system of Solvency II is structured around three pillars: the first concerns the quantitative requirements of prudential supervision; the second the qualitative requirements (corporate governance, internal control and risk management) and the supervisory activity; and the third looks at the issue of information and market discipline (supervisory reporting and public disclosure) (Von Bomhard 2005; Buckham et al. 2010).

The first pillar, in addition to setting out criteria for investments and asset and liability evaluation, contains provisions relating to the calculation of capital requirements.

The supervisory regime requires that the undertaking hold sufficient own funds to cover the SCR calculated on the basis of the assumption of business continuity.

The requirement is calibrated so as to guarantee that all quantified risks to which the undertaking is exposed are taken into consideration; its measurement is used to guarantee a level of capital that allows the insurer to absorb significant unexpected losses while offering the insured the reasonable certainty that payments will be fully honoured at maturity.

Operatively, the SCR must consider how much capital is necessary to cope with all commitments undertaken over a period of one year, given a specific confidence level (99.5%). In other words, this corresponds to the Value at Risk (VaR) of the company's own funds; as a result of this, all significant and quantifiable risks to which the company is exposed (underwriting, market, credit, operational and liquidity risks) must be factored into and counted in the calculation.

The SCR calculation may use a standard formula, or make use of an internal model, whether total or partial, which best reflects the specific business risk profile.

Solvency II not only seeks to ensure companies have the appropriate capital requirements to face various business risks; it also aims to encourage insurers to develop a genuine business risk culture. To this end, the supervisory approach pushes companies to substitute the standard SCR calculation methods with internal models that more precisely gather the interdependencies between risk categories. On this note, the supervisory authorities have the power to force companies to develop an internal model, either complete or partial, when the standard formula does not correctly reflect the company's risk profile (Cappiello 2018). Essentially, the less coherent the individual company's risk profile is with the assumptions made at the basis of the standardised method, the more preferential the use of internal models should be when quantifying risks. Obviously, it will be in a company's best interest to adopt internal models whenever its specific risk profile leads to the development of a capital requirement that is lower than the result of the standard formula.

It goes without saying that companies that use advanced risk management systems alongside adequate risk mitigation and/or diversification techniques are at an advantage in terms of capital requirements compared to companies distinguished by higher risk profiles.

All risks to which a company is exposed cannot always be adequately identified and defined through quantitative measures only; therefore the second pillar envisaged by Solvency II is formed, in the first instance, by regulations that concern governance, risk management and the internal control systems of the company, and secondly, by the regulation of the activities, tools and supervisory powers.

Specifically, pillar 2 contains the requirements regarding the way the undertaking should be organised. As part of pillar 2, all insurance undertakings are required to have in place an effective system of governance with written policies in relation to the risk governance system, the internal control and organisation of the undertaking. An effective risk management system covers all material risks and requires, among others, an appropriate own risk and solvency assessment (ORSA) (see Chapter 4).

In conclusion, the third pillar deals with the distribution of information and transparency in order to strengthen market mechanisms and risk-based supervisory mechanisms.

A standardised system of communication between insurance undertakings and supervisory authorities is an important element in the European Union's legislative framework. The system transcends simple financial communications and includes various types of information—usually confidential—required by a supervisory authority in order to fulfil its specific functions.

Moreover, it is possible to observe that transparency and public disclosure serve to strengthen the mechanisms and regulation of the market, i.e. the market's ability to assess the solvency of insurance undertakings.

Specifically, the aspects linked to market reporting obligations concern governance, risk management, solvency position and any breach of the capital requirements.

As we can see, in a certain sense the third pillar is the logical consequence of the first two pillars. As a matter of fact, the system seems to find an ideal complement in the fact that once the undertaking's level of risk is surveyed and assessed (first pillar) and after having monitored it through the appropriate infrastructure (second pillar), it transparently notifies the market of its static and dynamic status.

4.3 Evolutionary Traits of the Solvency Regime in the USA

In the United States, the National Association of Insurance Commissioners (NAIC) is the national standard-setting organisation created and governed by the chief insurance regulators from the 50 states, the District of Columbia, and five US territories. It coordinates the work of the state insurance regulators that are responsible for insurance supervision, provides regulatory support to state insurance departments, and coordinates changes to insurance regulatory requirements (DeFrain 2012; FIO 2013).

The NAIC's solvency regime uses a risk-based capital (RBC) method of measuring the minimum amount of capital appropriate for a reporting entity, to support its overall business operations in consideration of its size and risk profile.

Before RBC was created, regulators used fixed capital standards as a primary tool for monitoring the financial solvency of insurance companies. Under fixed capital standards, owners are required to supply the same minimum amount of capital, regardless of the financial condition of the company. The requirements required by the states ranged from $500,000 to $6 million and was dependent upon the state and the line of business that an insurance carrier wrote. Companies had to meet these minimum capital and surplus requirements in order to be licensed and write business in the state. As insurance companies changed and grew, it became clear that the fixed capital standards were no longer effective in providing a sufficient cushion for many insurers.

The adoption of the RBC regime was driven by a string of large-company insolvencies that occurred in late 1980s and early 1990s. The NAIC established a working group to look at the feasibility of developing a statutory risk-based capital requirement for insurers. The RBC regime was created to provide a capital adequacy standard that is related to risk, raises a safety net for insurers, is uniform among the states, and provides regulatory authority for timely action (Broome and Markham 2000).

The RBC formula is primarily factor-based and considers all risks that are quantifiable and material for the industry, i.e. the framework typically covers all risks to some degree even if they are not explicitly reflected within the calculation of required capital. RBC is a laddered intervention framework that is designed to identify weakly capitalised companies and provide for an increasing degree of supervisory intervention based on the company's RBC level.

It has two main components: (1) the risk-based capital formula, that established a hypothetical minimum capital level that is compared to a company's actual capital level, and (2) a risk-based capital model law that grants automatic authority to the state insurance regulator to take specific actions based on the level of impairment (American Academy of Actuaries 2008).

The Risk-Based Capital Formula was developed as an additional tool to assist regulators in the financial analysis of insurance companies. The purpose of the formula is to establish a minimum capital requirement based on the types of risks to which a company is exposed. Separate RBC models have been developed for each of the primary insurance types: Life, Property/Casualty, Health and Fraternal. This reflects the differences in the economic environments facing these companies.

The risk factors for the NAIC's RBC formulas focus on three major areas: (1) Asset Risk; (2) Underwriting Risk and (3) Other Risk. The emphasis on these risks differs from one formula to the next. As a generic formula, every single risk exposure of a company is not necessarily captured in the formula. The formula focuses on the material risks that are common for the particular insurance type. For example, interest rate risk is included in the Life RBC formula because the risk of losses due to changes in interest rate levels is a material risk for many life insurance products.

Strategic risk, reputational risk and currency risk are not explicitly accounted for in the RBC. The factors of the formula are derived from historical industry-wide data, while internal models are used for interest rate and market risk only. In the US solvency regime, an internal model is typically understood to be a quantitative requirement that employs a company-specific actuarial cash-flow projection and is contrasted with formula reserves and factor-based capital charges, which are uniform for all companies. Thus, internal model application, using prescribed parameters and time horizons, is limited to specific products in the life RBC formula and will be utilised in the catastrophe risk module currently under development for P/C insurers. For the (limited) cases where partial internal models are allowed for life insurance, these models do not require supervisory approval as regulatory minimum/floor scenarios persist. However, the regulators review internal models as part of the ongoing solvency surveillance process.

Under the RBC system, regulators have the authority and statutory mandate to take preventive and corrective measures that vary depending on the capital deficiency indicated by the RBC result. These measures are designed to provide for early regulatory intervention to correct problems before insolvencies become inevitable, thereby minimising the number and adverse impact of insolvencies.

The RBC formula generates the regulatory minimum amount of capital that a company is required to maintain to avoid regulatory action. There are four levels of action that a company can trigger under the formula: company action, regulatory action, authorised control and mandatory control levels. Each RBC level requires some particular action on the part of the regulator, the company, or both. For example, an insurer that breaches the Company Action Level must produce a plan to restore its RBC levels. This could include adding capital, purchasing reinsurance, reducing the amount of insurance it writes, or pursuing a merger or acquisition.

The NAIC's RBC system operates as a tripwire system that gives regulators clear legal authority to intervene in the business affairs of an insurer that triggers one of the action levels specified in the RBC law. As a tripwire system, RBC alerts regulators to undercapitalised companies while there is still time for the regulators to react quickly and effectively to minimise the overall costs associated with insolvency. In addition, the RBC results may be used to intervene when a company is found to be in hazardous condition in the course of an examination.

In the wake of Solvency II regime, over the past years, the NAIC has, as part of the Solvency Modernization Initiative (SMI), introduced reforms related to group supervision, corporate governance, enterprise risk management, liability valuation for life and annuity products (principle-based reserving) and reinsurance. In addition, as a result of the Dodd–Frank Act, the Federal Reserve has obtained supervisory powers concerning insurers that have been designated as systemically important as well as those holding company systems with a bank or thrift included within their structure (Mason 2015; Holzmuller 2009).

The NAIC adopted the Corporate Governance Annual Disclosure Model Act in 2014, requiring insurers to disclose their corporate governance framework. The annual disclosure includes policies and practices of the insurer's board and significant committees, policies and practices of senior management, and oversight of critical risk areas. ORSA is a new requirement for large insurers and insurance groups from 2015 (collectively the entities required to perform an ORSA make up over 90% of the United States premium volume). The ORSA includes an internal assessment of the risks associated with the insurer's current and projected future business plan, and an assessment is required of the sufficiency of capital resources to support those risks in both the current and stressed environments. At a minimum, three major components are required: (1) a description of the insurer's risk management framework, (2) the insurer's assessment of risk exposure and (3) the group risk capital and prospective solvency assessment.

5 Conclusions

Historically, the main purpose of intervention by a public authority was to make decisions regarding regulations on the guarantee and control of company solvency, in addition to the measures used to reduce the negative social and economic impact deriving from events subsequent to the insolvency of that insurance company.

In recognition of the evolving risk landscape, insurance solvency regimes around the globe are currently undergoing significant changes. Jurisdictions in the North and South American, European and Asia-Pacific regions have reviewed or are reviewing their solvency regimes in order to enhance policyholder protection and financial stability (Sharara et al. 2010). Although there is much common ground with regard to the main elements of existing and developing solvency regimes, it is clear that these common elements are interpreted and/or applied in different ways, taking account of differences in regulatory or supervisory practices.

The project for the risk-based global insurance standard—substantially the same across world jurisdictions—which is currently under development by the International Association of Insurance Supervisors (IAIS 2004, 2005, 2019), is likely to bear upon these principles while attempting to cope with the challenges of harmonising multi-jurisdictional regulations, specific products jurisdiction or corporate law requirements at a global level. Significant achievements will be made possible by a shared commitment from the world's insurance supervisors to the maintenance of fair, safe and stable insurance markets for the benefit and protection of policyholders.

References

American Academy of Actuaries. (2008, September). *C3 Life and Annuity Capital Work Group*. Presentation to the National Association of Insurance Commissioners Life Risk Based Capital, Work Group.

Arnott, R., & Stiglitz, J. (1991). *Equilibrium in Competitive Insurance Markets with Moral Hazard* (National Bureau of Economic Research Working Paper Series, n. 3588).

Arrow, K. J. (1970). *Insurance, Risk and Resource Allocation*. In K. J. Arrow (Ed.), *Essay in the Theory of Risk Bearing*. Amsterdam: North-Holland.

Bianchi, T. (1975). *Le banche di deposito*. Torino: Utet.

Boadway, R., Leite-Monteiro, M., Marchand, M., & Pestieau, P. (2014). *Social Insurance and Redistribution with Moral Hazard and Adverse Selection* (Discussion Paper Series). Centre for Economic Policy, Research n. 4253.

Borch, K. H., Sandmo, A., & Aase, K. K. (1990). *Economics of Insurance*. Amsterdam: North-Holland.

Broome, L., & Markham, J. W. (2000). Banking and Insurance: Before and After the Gramm-Leach-Bliley Act. *The Journal of Corporation Law, 25*, 723–786.

Buckham, D., Wahl, J., Munagala, S., & Rose, S. (2010). *Executive's Guide to Solvency II*. Hoboken, NJ: Wiley.

Cappiello, A. (2018). *L'attività asicurativa. Regole, gestione, business models*. Milano: Franco Angeli.

Cassandro, P. E. (1975). *Le gestioni assicuratrici*. Torino: Utet.

CoSO—Committee of Sponsoring Organizations of the Treadway Commission. (1992). *Internal Control over Financial Reporting*.

CoSO—Committee of Sponsoring Organizations of the Treadway Commission (2013). *Internal Control—Integrated Framework*.

De Finetti, B., & Emanuelli, F. (1967). *Economia delle assicurazioni*. Torino: Utet.

DeFrain, K. (2012, January). *US Insurance Financial Regulatory Oversight and the Role of Capital Requirements*. NAIC Center for Insurance and Policy Research. http://www.naic.org/cipr_newsletter_archive/vol2_oversight.htm.

De Haan, J., Oosterloo, S., & Schoenmaker, D. (2015). *Financial Markets and Institutions: A European Perspective*. Cambridge: Cambridge University Press.

Dionne, G., Fombaron, N., & Doherty, N. (2012). *Adverse Selection in Insurance Contracting*. Available at https://ssrn.com/abstract=2132555.

Doff, R. (2016). The Final Solvency II Framework: Will It Be Effective? *The Geneva Papers on Risk and Insurance—Issues and Practice, 41*(4), 587–607.

D'Onza, G. (2008). *Il sistema di controllo interno nella prospettiva del risk management*. Milano: Giuffrè.

Eling, M., Schmeiser, H., & Schmit, J. T. (2007). The Solvency II Process: Overview and Critical Analysis. *Risk Management and Insurance Review, 10*(1), 69–85.

European Commission. (2002, December). *Report on the Prudential Supervision of Insurance Undertakings* (Sharma Report), Conference of Insurance Supervisory Services of the Member States of the European Union.

European Commission. (2007, July). *Proposal for a Directive of the European Parliament and of the Council on the Taking-Up and Pursuit of the Business of Insurance and Reinsurance*, Brussels.

EIOPA—European Insurance and Occupational Pensions Authority. (2018). *Failures and Near Misses in Insurance* (pp. 1–52). Luxembourg.

FIO—Federal Insurance Office. (2013, December). *How to Modernize and Improve the System Insurance Regulation in the United States*, Report.

Finkelstein, A. (2015). *Moral Hazard in Health Insurance*. New York: Columbia University Press.

Gupta, P. (2006, September). COSO 1992 Control Framework and Management Reporting on Internal Control: Survey and Analysis of Implementation Practices. *Strategic Finance*, 27–33.

Handel, B. R. (2013). Adverse Selection and Inertia in Health Insurance Markets: When Nudging Hurts. *American Economic Review, 103*(7), 2643–2682.

Heisen, P., Kilian, A., Lötgerink, C., & Weirich, M. (2014). Solvency II, the Practical Implications for Asset Managers and Insurers. *PwC*. Available at https://www.pwc.nl/nl/assets/documents/pwc-memo-solvency-ii.pdf.

Holzmuller I. (2009). The United States RBC Standards, Solvency II and the Swiss Solvency Test: A Comparative Assessment. *The Geneva Papers, 34*, 56–77.

Hull, J. C. (2018). *Risk Management and Financial Institutions*. Hoboken, NJ: Wiley.

Insurance Europe. (2014). *Why Insurers Differ from Banks* (pp. 1–60). Brussels.

IAIS—International Association of Insurance Supervisors. (2004, October). *A New Framework for Insurance Supervision: Towards a Common Structure and Common Standards for the Assessment of Insurance Solvency*.

IAIS—International Association of Insurance Supervisors. (2005, October). *Towards a Common Structure and Common Standards for the Assessment of Insurance Solvency: Cornerstones for the Formulation of Regulatory Financial Requirements*.

IAIS—International Association of Insurance Supervisors. (2019, November). *Insurance Core Principles. And Common Framework for the Supervision of Internationally Active Insurance Groups*.

Kasturi, R. (2006). Performance Management in Insurance Corporation. *Journal of Business Administration, 5*(1), 1–30.

Kessler, D. (2008). Insurance Market Mechanism and Government Interventions. *Journal of Banking & Finance, 32*, 4–14.

Kesternich, I., & Schumacher, H. (2014). On the Use of Information in Oligopolistic Insurance Markets. *Journal of Risk and Insurance, 81*(1), 159–175.

Krischanitz, C. (2013). *Comparison of the Regulatory Approach in Insurance and Banking in the Context of Solvency II* (pp. 1–23). Brussels, Belgium: European Actuarial Consultative Group.

Mason, J. R. (2015, June). *Overview and Structure of Financial Supervision and Regulation in the US.* European Parliament, Policy Department A. 1–54.

Mishkin, F., & Eakins, S. (2018). *Financial Markets and Institutions.* Harlow, UK: Pearson Education.

Olajide, S. (2013). Corporate Governance and Insurance Company Growth: Challenges and Opportunities. *International Journal of Academic Research in Economics and Management Sciences, 2*(1), 286–305.

Outreville, J. F. (1998). *Theory and Practice of Insurance.* Boston: Kluwer Academic.

Ozigbo, A., & Orife, O. (2011). Internal Control and Fraud Prevention in Insurances Business. *International Journal of Economic Development, Research and Investment, 2*(3), 77.

Paci, S. (1979). L'intermediazione finanziaria delle imprese di assicurazione, *Bancaria*, 2/3.

Paci, S. (2004). Evoluzione della vigilanza assicurativa. *Rivista Diritto Ed Economia Delle Assicurazioni, 4,* 8–20.

Rothschild, M., & Stiglitz, J. (1976). Equilibrium in Competitive Insurance Markets: An Essay on the Economics of Imperfect Information. *Quarterly Journal of Economics, 90,* 629–649.

Santoboni F. (Ed.). (2017). *Manuale di gestione assicurativa.* Milano: Wolters Kluwer.

Sharara, I., Hardy, M., & Saunders, D. (2010). *A Comparative Analysis of U.S., Canadian and Solvency II Capital Adequacy Requirements in Life Insurance,* Society of Actuaries, All Rights Reserved, University of Waterloo.

Spencer, P. D. (2000). *The Structure and Regulation of Financial Markets.* Oxford: Oxford University Press.

Van Rossum, A. (2005). Regulation and Insurance Economics. *The Geneva Papers on Risk and Insurance—Issues and Practice, 30*(1), 43–46.

Von Bomhard, N. (2005). Risk and Capital Management in Insurance Companies. *The Geneva Papers on Risk and Insurance—Issue and Practice, 30,* 52–59.

CHAPTER 3

An Integrated Approach to Risk Governance in the Insurance Industry

Abstract The chapter highlights how the functional specialisation increases risk governance complexity of insurance intermediaries. This requires the development of a stronger risk oversight according to an enterprise risk management approach which enables firms to manage a wide array of risks in an integrated, enterprise-wide fashion. In this way, Enterprise Risk Management can contribute to generating significant value for insurance companies. The chapter ends by focusing on an integrated approach to classification, assessment, management and control of the various risks faced by the insurance activity (life and non-life): not only underwriting and reserve risk—typical of the insurance activity—but also market risk, credit risk, liquidity risk, operational risk and compliance risk.

Keywords Risk governance · Risk management · Enterprise risk management · Insurance risk · Underwriting risk · Reserve risk · Credit risk · Liquidity risk · Operational risk · Compliance risk

1 Introduction

The need to rely on a strategic approach to risk governance, including for regulatory purposes, requires the use of increasingly sophisticated integrated and systemic enterprise risk management methods.

A. Cappiello, *The European Insurance Industry*,
https://doi.org/10.1007/978-3-030-43142-6_3

It is useful, in this respect, to refer to the Enterprise Risk Management—Integrated Framework published by the Committee of Sponsoring Organizations (CoSO) of the Treadway Commission in 2004 (CoSO 2004) and revised in 2017 (CoSO 2017), as an evolutionary model of the CoSO Internal Control Integrated Framework (1992) and the New CoSO Framework (2013).

The CoSO defines Enterprise Risk Management as a process used to allow for effective identification, assessment and management of the different types of risk to which the undertaking is exposed during its activities, which involves all company personnel. This process describes the methods for virtuous risk management intended to identify potential events that might influence the company's operations, to keep the risk within tolerable limits and provide reasonable assurance regarding the achievement of the business objectives.

The definition of ERM offered by the CoSO is deliberately general, liable to wide application and inclusive of key concepts to guide risk management in an integrated manner.

The successful application of the various stages in this process brings benefits for the company in terms of risk management and therefore in terms of developing its policies, since it creates value and protects the company assets by aligning the risk appetite with the strategy while developing actions in response to risk, thereby minimising the effects deriving from unexpected events, identifying and managing risks with impacts on different organisational areas, seizing business opportunities and streamlining capital needs.

Enterprise Risk Management, as an integral part of corporate governance, is a process that involves the Board of Directors, the management team and other individuals in the corporate structure. It ranges from the strategic and decision-making phase, extending subjectively across the entire production organisation, which is involved in the analysis, assessment and readiness of the most convenient risk measurements.

The model in question, finding support in the now characteristic components of the 1992 CoSO Internal Control Integrated Framework—internal control environment, risk assessment, control activities, information flows and monitoring—sets out the phases in which the risk management process is expressed, linking it more clearly to the company mission and objectives fixed beforehand.

The entity objectives are set forth in following four categories: (i) Strategic—high-level goals, aligned with and supporting its mission; (ii) Operations—effective and efficient use of its resources; (iii) Reporting—reliability of reporting; and (iv) Compliance—compliance with applicable laws and regulations. These objectives, albeit formulated from a general standpoint, are channelled into the same company mission or, in any case, are expressions of the management team's decisions in light of value creation for the stakeholders.

2 An Integrated Approach to Insurance Risks Management

Though the assumption of risks transferred to it by other economies constitutes its core business, the insurance undertaking is itself exposed to uncertainty. Therefore, over time the management team must define the level of uncertainty that the undertaking can accept, i.e. the level of vulnerability compatible with the value creation objectives.

The uncertainty that the insurance undertaking's management must face is manifested in the dual value of opportunities and risks, which potentially compete in increasing or decreasing the value of production, respectively. It follows that the company's management, with a view to maximising the objective, is requested to identify, assess and draw benefits from the former and, by contrast, to identify and contain the losses and costs of the latter.

These are the premises on which enterprise risk management is based, including in insurance undertakings, by virtue of which the Board, when deciding on the objectives and strategies, the management team, while pursuing the latter to achieve the former and, in general, every party appointed to perform the management processes, identify the risks that may prevent the achievement of the business purpose, then assess the risks with a view to managing and containing them within the acceptable level of vulnerability.

Risk governance, defined as the framework of rules, relationships, systems and processes within organisations with regard to the management and control of risk, represents the founding element of a solid and effective enterprise risk management (ERM) process (FSB 2013).

In contrast to traditional silo-based risk approach—with which companies managed risks arising from their business units separately in each unit, enterprise risk management process enables insurance undertaking to approach risks in an enterprise-wide, consolidated, structured, dynamic and continuous way with a long-term perspective while taking into account a firm's strategy, all employees, its knowledge base, processes and technologies (Colquitt et al. 1999; Dickinson 2001; Kleffner et al. 2003; Beasley et al. 2005; Hoyt and Liebenberg 2011; Altuntas et al. 2012). Due to the incorporation of risk management within corporate strategy, ERM must be a top-down directed process (instead of a mid-level technical function) with responsibility at the Board level (Aebi et al. 2012; Nair et al. 2014).

ERM encompasses activities and strategies which enable the company to identify, measure, reduce or exploit, as well as to control and monitor the exposure to various types of corporate risks for the purpose of increasing the organisation's value to its stakeholders.

A number of studies on firms' decisions to start an ERM programme provide evidence that firms adopt ERM for direct economic benefits (Liebenberg and Hoyt 2003; Pagach and Warr 2011; Altuntas et al. 2012), and that ERM is associated with improvements in firm performance and increases in firm value (Hoyt and Liebenberg 2011; Eckles et al. 2014; Farrell and Gallagher 2015; Grace et al. 2015) by creating synergies between different risk management activities, increasing capital efficiency, avoiding the underinvestment problem in financially restricted firms, and by reducing the cost of external financing.

More broadly, ERM is said to promote increased risk awareness that facilitates better operational and strategic decision-making.

For ERM to bring benefits, as is explained thoroughly in the existing ERM literature (Cumming and Hirtle 2001; Lam 2001; Meulbroek 2002; Liebenberg and Hoyt 2003; Beasley et al. 2005; Nocco and Stulz 2006), it should be integrated in the most important business processes, such as strategic management, strategic planning, as well as in finance and investment decisions in order to ensure the consistent evaluation and management of risks that arise from business initiatives and plans.

The fundamental improvements of enterprise-wide risk management approaches are, to some extent, also induced by regulatory pressure in the wake of the implementation of Solvency II.

The risk-based regulatory approach of the first and second pillars of Solvency II incorporates many of the principles of risk governance including stronger risk oversight at Board level, stronger risk accountability in the senior management team and promotion of a risk culture. The development of the risk culture, i.e. a system of shared values and common regulations created in the undertaking in order to protect it from the risks to which it is exposed, is indeed fundamental for risk management, provided that said culture makes it possible to acquire awareness of the risks, communicate the information obtained during their assessment and contribute to their management in an effective and efficient way.

Solvency II requires an integrated, enterprise-wide perspective of a firm's entire risk portfolio, in contrast to traditional silo-based risk management approaches, and the risk management system has to be consistent with the company's overall business strategy (Gatzert and Wesker 2012; Bohnert et al. 2019).

Regardless of the need to comply with Solvency II requirements, several studies highlight how the implementation of an ERM process also specifically contribute to generating significant value for insurance companies (Meulbroek 2002; Liebenberg and Hoyt 2003; Beasley et al. 2005, 2009; Hoyt and Liebenberg 2011; McShane et al. 2011; Pagach and Warr 2011; Aebi et al. 2012; Altuntas et al. 2011, 2012; Baxter et al. 2013; Farrell and Gallagher 2015; Lechner and Gatzert 2018; Ai et al. 2018).

ERM in insurance companies is also recognised by rating agencies such as Standard & Poor's or A.M. Best in their overall rating procedures (Hoyt and Liebenberg 2011; Eckles et al. 2014).

A.M. Best began to implement its Enterprise Risk Model for US insurers in late 2001 (A.M. Best 2001). Standard and Poor's introduced ERM analysis into its global corporate credit rating process for financial and insurance companies in 2005 in order to evaluate both the financial strength and creditworthiness of insurance companies (S&P 2005, 2013; Berry-Stölzle and Xu 2018). It is assumed that insurance companies with improved ratings are able to achieve higher premiums due to enhanced security levels or reduced inefficiencies over the course of the individual risk assessment, thus helping firms to achieve higher overall returns (McShane et al. 2010).

A fair and integrated identification and assessment of risk requires the continuous collection of data regarding the internal, external, existing and prospective risks the undertaking may incur during its activities, transversally involving all operating processes and functional areas (Floreani 2005). Therefore not only underwriting and reserve risk—typical of the insurance activity—but also market risk, credit risk, liquidity risk, operational and compliance risk are taken into account.

2.1 *The Technical-Actuarial Risk Management*

Technical-actuarial risk, specific to the insurance sector, derives from deviations between the starting statistical hypotheses, used as a basis for the premium calculation, and the effective frequency of occurrence of the risks insured and average size of the claims to be paid (Back and Skipper 1994; Babbel and Santomero 1997). This risk, therefore, must be considered as the sum of the underwriting risk and reserve risk.

As is obvious, the risk depending on the variability of the results may have positive or negative consequences in that it generates an advantage or damage for insurance management.

Forecasting errors are the general cause for the undertaking's economic fluctuations; these may derive from a lack of information, i.e. insufficient availability of historical data relating to events requiring forecast, or even by inadequate processing or weighting of the data held. In this hypothesis, these risks of error may be considered subjective to a certain extent (Marrison 2002).

Another cause for risk must be attributed to the trend of the hypothesised events which is significantly different from the one used as a basis for the forecasts. In this respect, we refer to objective deviations: while the prediction was made by adopting reliable and correct bases, this may be contradicted by the events' tangible evolution being completely different from the one generated according to experience, albeit extensive.

In the insurance undertaking, whose activity is mainly founded on statistical data, subjective errors are less likely to occur, though they cannot be excluded entirely. As a matter of fact, various risks exist, especially ones that fall under the non-life business, for which the statistical bases available are not particularly widespread. Equally, a certain level of subjectivity is nevertheless always present in the appreciation of each risk's characteristics—obvious or otherwise—that may lead to incorrect assessments during underwriting with false selection issues.

With particular reference to assessing the technical provisions, the management phase of the assumed risk also implies situations of subjectivity.

In any case, objective errors are more frequent, since it is easily stated that the trend of the insured events does not always reflect what is indicated by the statistics. Faced with phenomena that present a certain constancy over time, there are in fact others that undergo more or less pronounced changes, and that record rather consistent deviations, either negative or positive, between the effective frequency of the claims and the frequency used as the basis for the premium calculations and resulting from the statistics available to the insurer.

It is noted, in this regard, that the insurance undertaking's technical costs are affected to a minor extent, in comparison to the economies of other intermediaries, by the economic events and performance of some related variables, whereas they are greatly influenced by unexpected events—non-life especially—no matter how appropriately assessed and constantly monitored by the company using statistical and probabilistic bases.

The circumstances that modify the average frequency and/or average size of the claims may be attributed to objective causes, as well as the moral hazard behaviours of the insured, tending obviously to exacerbate the risk.

In summary, the negative deviations attributable to the technical risk derive from problems of under-pricing, i.e. by problems of excessive claims, or even by the inadequacy of the technical provisions.

The under-pricing risk may depend on the insurance undertaking's voluntary or involuntary behaviours.

In the first case the company, with the intention of maintaining or extending its market share, consciously engages prices (premium rates) that are not in line with the underlying actuarial hypothesis. Rate liberalisation, by releasing companies from supervisory control, may contribute to accentuating this type of risk.

The second hypothesis occurs when there is a gap between the expected claims and effective claims (properly referred to as the risk of over claiming), or when there are deviations from the hypotheses of the return on investment or estimate of the management costs considered in the formation of the rates.

In the non-life business the risk of over claiming, which concerns both the estimated frequency of the claims as well as their average cost, may be attributed to various factors, such as: the dispersion of the distribution of claims by number and amount (normal deviations); fluctuations due to exceptional situations of the risk level performance, linked for example to catastrophes (exceptional deviations); changes in the social, economic or technological conditions in the factors that affect the frequency or monetary extent of claims (systematic deviations).

In the life business the risk of over claiming is linked to the assessment of the demographic risk connected to some phenomena such as extended life expectancy, unfavourable variations in estimated mortality, abandonment of contracts and surrender of policies which reduce the number of policies in the portfolio with a subsequent increase in the random fluctuations of mortality.

An additional technical risk concerns the assessment of the technical provisions which may prove inconsistent with the obligations assumed. In addition to incorrect estimates by the company, this may also depend on changes in the context of reference that tend to exacerbate the amount of compensation due.

Other technical risks relate to the risk of loading, or to the risk connected to an excessive production growth associated with a scarce selection of risks or insufficient equity.

In the context of Solvency II, the non-life insurance risk, deriving from the uncertainty connected to the technical risks assumed, is split into the following risk sub-modules:

1. *Premium and reserve risk*: deriving from fluctuations relating to the moment of occurrence, the frequency and severity of the insured events in addition to the moment of occurrence and amount of the claims payments. In this case, a joint calculation is made for the premium risk which reflects the risk that the premiums are not sufficient to cover the claims and costs, and for the reserve risk, which, related to the existing policies, is determined by the risk that the reserves are not sufficient against future payments;
2. *Non-life catastrophe risk* (*CAT risk*): deriving from a significant uncertainty of the hypotheses regarding fixing prices and establishing reserves in relation to extreme or exceptional events that are not adequately captured by the premium and reserve risk.

On the other hand, life assurance risk is traced back to the uncertainty connected to the following risks:

1. *Mortality risk*: deriving from variations in the level, trend or volatility of mortality rates, where an increase in the mortality rate gives rise to an increase in the insurance liabilities' value;
2. *Longevity risk*: deriving from variations in the level, trend or volatility of mortality rates, where a decrease in the mortality rate gives rise to an increase in the insurance liabilities' value;

3. *Disability-morbidity risk*: deriving from variations in the level, trend or volatility of disability, health and morbidity rates;
4. *Lapse risk*: deriving from variations in the level or volatility of the lapse rates, withdrawals, renewals and surrender of policies;
5. *Life expense risk*: deriving from variations in the level, trend or volatility of the expenses incurred in relation to the insurance or reinsurance contracts;
6. *Life catastrophe risk*: deriving from the significant uncertainty of the hypotheses regarding fixing prices and establishing provisions in relation to extreme or sporadic events;
7. *Review risk*: deriving from fluctuations in the level, trend or volatility of the review rates of the returns, due to variations in the judicial framework or state of health of the insured person.

Lastly, the health risks are divided into: *expense risk*, *premium reserve risk* and *epidemic risk*. The latter reflects the risk of loss or unfavourable variation in the insurance liabilities' value, deriving from the significant uncertainty of the hypotheses relating to fixing prices or establishing the technical provisions in relation to significant epidemics and to the unusual accumulation of risks in extreme circumstances.

While acknowledging the implementation of an effective internal control system to transversally control the risks in every activity area, specifically, the techniques adopted for the management of the technical and actuarial risk are attributable, as an initial approximation, to the policies of selection/prevention of risks and the diversification of the insurance portfolio, which are joined by the various risk hedging operations.

Generally, the risk selection involves a risk classification process, so as to determine the premium in proportion to the risk assumed, excluding the risks deemed unacceptable due to their extent or the lack of knowledge regarding the probability of occurrence.

The need to adjust the premiums to the unique characteristics of the risks assumed is obvious, though this adjustment must be considered broadly, since it would be exceedingly costly to take account of all profiles of each individual risk. Nevertheless, a better determination of the general premium, established by risk class, may be pursued by requiring that the insured party adopt some security measures to reduce both the risk's extent and probability of occurrence, thus making it easier for the undertaking to manage it. The insertion of particular contractual limitations also aims to attenuate the risk assumed by the undertaking: we refer to the clauses that envisage the fixing of deductibles, waiting periods, etc.

Let us also consider that insurance undertakings, when determining premium rates, follow the principle of applying a margin—loading risk—that takes account of the possible negative deviations between the effective and expected claims frequency. However, calculating these margins is no simple feat since it must be done in a preventive manner and on empirical bases; it does not seem convenient, among other things, to apply rather high margins that would inadequately increase the size of the premium with evident negative effects in business terms.

When tackling actuarial insurance risks, the diversification/fractioning of the risk portfolio is particularly important.

Portfolio diversification is one of the mechanisms aiming to rebalance the portfolio composition, looked at from a strategic medium- to long-term perspective. The decisions to diversify the risky liabilities are made at geographic level, counterparty level and at the level of large types of insurance branches, according to criteria intended to create portfolio combinations with overall claims performances that are independent or negatively correlated; this is done in the aim of reducing the overall risk and stabilising business profitability.

Rebalancing the liabilities portfolio may also be achieved by the transfer of the risk, either partial or total, through reinsurance or securitisation transactions, or by using innovative financial instruments such as catastrophe derivatives or financial derivatives.

Considered particularly useful for catastrophe-related risks, securitisation allows for the transfer of technical risks to the capital market through unique financial instruments, such as catastrophe bonds, which, faced with high returns, allow for the insurance undertaking's financing in relation to the negative event's occurrence. In this regard, both the payment of interest and the return of capital are subject to the non-occurrence of the catastrophic event.

Catastrophe derivatives, on the other hand, offer protection against catastrophe risks in the event of insufficient liquidity by the insurance or reinsurance undertaking. These include catastrophe futures—which allow for hedging against increases in the claims rate above the system average—and catastrophe options, which, following payment of a premium, make it possible to purchase an insurance future in the event that the average number of claims increases.

We must not overlook, in this regard, that in addition to using the instruments just mentioned, the insurance undertaking may seek to stabilise the economic performance of the management through recourse to various strategies of agreement and collaboration with similar undertakings, including all the various forms of aggregate strategies attributable to the concentration and/or integration process that is now particularly important.

As we can see, operation through a group, hence facilitating infra-business relationships between insurance undertakings from various branches and insurance undertakings and reinsurance undertakings and enlarging the operational bases and related turnover, allows for a simpler distribution and compensation of the risks—with greater facility of verifying the law of large numbers—and therefore of economic result stabilisation.

2.2 *The Market Risk Management*

In its dual role as risk as well as financial intermediary, the insurance undertaking is subject to market risks, i.e. risks relating to price, interest rate and foreign exchange.

The price risk relates to both changes in the premium rate on the insurance market, those concerning the prices of the financial instruments on the financial market, as well as those of exchange rates.

Market risk is managed by the directors of the business units appointed to manage the insurance/reinsurance processes and takes place alongside the management of the technical-actuarial risk.

Exposure to foreign exchange risk derives from diversity in the currencies in which the assets and liabilities are expressed and the correlated revenues and costs, with repercussions on the extent of the profits and capital.

The aforesaid risk may be hedged through the creation (as is normal for Italian insurance undertakings) of a near-perfect matching between the currency of denomination of the policies stipulated and that of the assets acquired to hedge the technical provisions.

In the limits within which the currency risk cannot be or is not conveniently manageable with said methods, the insurance undertaking may use derivatives such as swaps, futures and options.

On the other hand, the interest risk is identified in an intermediary's vulnerability to variations in the market rates; this must be assessed in the dual aspect of "investment risk" and "income risk".

The former is seen in the change in value of the securities portfolio induced by variations in the rates. However, this risk cannot be defined as specific to financial intermediaries, since it affects any investor in transferable securities.

Income risk arises in relation to the mismatches existing between assets and liabilities that render the two aggregates otherwise sensitive to variations in the market rates. The different possibility of adjustment to the performance of the negotiated asset and liability rates is attributable to diversity in the volumes, maturities, nature of the rates and contractual repricing conditions referring to the balance sheet assets and liabilities; hence the need to establish a convenient correlation between the two fundamental aggregates such as technical provisions and investments.

As maturity transformation is not prevalent in insurance industry—although present with varying levels of intensity depending on the business lines—the income risk derives mainly from the unique characteristics of intermediation, where many of the variables forming the contract (on which the price and amount of the insurance guarantee are determined) are pre-established in conditions of uncertainty and on the basis of estimates. In this sense, the income risk, largely attributable in other financial intermediaries to the interest risk, is composite in nature, where the interest rate forms only one component.

However, we must distinguish between the business lines that show clearly different sensitivities to interest risk (De Finetti and Emanuelli 1967).

It is noted first and foremost that by analogy with any investor, both types of insurers—life and non-life—are exposed to an investment risk referring to the financial asset portfolio.

Income risk, on the other hand, shows different intensities and characteristics according to each business line, and seems attributable to the role assumed by fixing an interest rate while defining the technical and economic characteristics that govern the insurance contracts. Particular reference is made to the relevance of the interest rate in the context of the contractual conditions, as well as the possibility to amend the benchmark rate in relation to the variability of the return rates of the assets and therefore following changes in the market rates (Daly and Kapel 2006).

It is known that the growing integration between actuarial and financial activity ensures that the results of the latter are decisive in the fixing of premiums, defined in advance also in relation to returns hypotheses deriving from the use of the technical provisions.

In the non-life business lines, however, rate risk generally only relates to the assets, and does not involve the liabilities since no guaranteed return rate is contractually fixed, though we must take this into implicit account when determining the premium. Let us also consider that the revaluation—usually annually—of contracts in non-life business lines, and therefore of the related premium rates, facilitates the amendment of the benchmark interest rates, rendering the interest rate risk less significant.

A typical example of rate risk referring to non-life insurance is given by the hypothesis of liabilities with a real indexing that envisages the variation of the cost of compensation based on inflation performance, which is contrasted by assets remunerated at a fixed rate or a rate with different indexing to that of the liabilities.

The extent of the interest rate risk is in any case more relevant in life insurance and capitalisation, given the savings component in some cases explicitly attributed to characteristic contracts (Gardner and Mills 1988). This is highlighted with reference to some types of policies offered; for example, in pure capitalisation contracts we find a genuine interest rate risk borne by the insurer.

Though the interest rate risk is limited by the practice of annually recognising the premium revaluation rate on the basis of the returns achieved by the asset management, it is also evident that said risk may be burdensome when a guaranteed minimum rate of return is granted and any guaranteed *plus* agreed contractually.

Evidently, interest risk arises in phases of falling rates, when the asset returns deviate unfavourably from those recognised on the contracts stipulated, and their duration is much longer. In fact, the recognition of a return rate in the above-mentioned terms constitutes an element of rigidity in the financial structure of the insurance undertaking, exposing it to the interest rate risk sometimes un-modifiable for the duration of the contract, is correlated with a rate of asset return that instead is affected by the performance of the market rates.

In order to tackle this risk level, which is intrinsically proportional to the insurance intermediation activity and also difficult to eliminate with reference to the length of time, companies usually use technical rates that are decisively lower than market ones, in line with the regulatory requirements. Furthermore, some conditions in the life-capitalisation products, such as the indexing of premiums or insured capital or profit sharing, may be interpreted as attempts, on the one hand, to grant the insured parties the advantages of fluctuating market returns, but also, on the other hand, of transferring the rate risk partly onto them.

In the Solvency II framework, the definition of the overall capital requirement against market risk takes account of the following risk submodules (Poufinas and Tsitsika 2018):

1. *Interest rate risk*, existing for all assets and liabilities and financial instruments whose value is sensitive to changes in the structure of the interest rates or their volatility;
2. *Equity risk*, relating to the assets and liabilities and the financial instruments whose value is sensitive to changes in the level or volatility of the capital instruments' market prices. This risk must capture the systemic risk (not containable through diversification), whereas the idiosyncratic equity risk is included in the concentration risk subcategory;
3. *Property risk*, specific to the assets and liabilities and the financial instruments whose value is sensitive to changes or volatility of real estate market price;
4. *Currency risk*, relating to the assets and liabilities and financial instruments sensitive to variations or volatility of foreign exchange rates;
5. *Spread risk*, relating to the assets, liabilities and financial instruments sensitive to variations in the level or volatility of the credit spread compared to the risk-free rates structure;
6. *Concentration risk*, relating to the additional risks for the insurance or reinsurance undertaking deriving from the lack of diversification of the assets portfolio or from large exposure to the risk of non-compliance by a single issuer of securities or a group of associated issuers.

For each "sub-risk", a capital requirement is determined. The capital requirement for market risk is determined by aggregating the sub-requirements according to a matrix of pre-established correlation that takes account of the benefit of diversification among the risk sources considered.

For the purposes of managing interest risk, special importance is held, especially with reference to the life insurance where there are medium- and long-term maturities, by asset and liability management (ALM), i.e. the simultaneous management of assets and liabilities. In this sense, it is possible to resort to typical ALM techniques such as cash flow analysis, duration analysis and scenario analysis.

The first measures exposure to interest rate risk by calculating the effect of changes in the market interest rates on the expected cash flows on the assets and liabilities; the duration analysis, through the use of duration models on the assets and liabilities, estimates the effects of the variability of market interest rates on the economic value of the net worth; lastly, the scenario analysis appraises the impact of variations in the market interest rates on the economic value of the net worth by predicting the changing dynamics of the cash flows of the assets and liabilities (Swiss Re 2000).

Hedging the interest rate risk may be tackled by making use of derivatives or forms of external hedging such as swaps, options and futures, used for the transfer of risks linked to variations in interest rates, exchange rates and the prices of shares, bonds and stock market indices, respect to which ALM provides indications on the methods of use for amending the characteristics of the financial instruments and, therefore, for objectives of interest rate risk readjustment and control.

2.3 *The Liquidity Risk Management*

As in all companies, including insurance, liquidity risk originates from mismatching between incoming and outgoing cash flows.

As an initial approximation, it is safe to state that insurers have traditionally been viewed as having less exposure to liquidity risk than banks as a result of differences in the business model—they receive premiums upfront and pay claims later—allowing them to maintain a pool of liquid assets in most standard activities. As a matter of fact, the functional characteristics, and in particular the inversion of the economic and financial cycle in insurance economies, increasing the occasions for substantial control over financial coordination, alongside the possibility to schedule monetary outflow (claims) within certain limits, tend to facilitate the governance of liquidity and attenuate its related risks, so that liquidity tensions would show an episodic nature requiring recourse to forms of external financing (direct and/or indirect) or unexpected and sudden disposal of the existing investments, made on the basis of complementarity or alternation between them in order to face claims.

At aggregate level, especially on the basis of statistical predictions and experience, the company should therefore be able to discover the economic and financial dynamics of its liabilities and subsequently predict the frequency of the outgoing cash flows and the degree of liquidity of the risk portfolio.

Nevertheless, the above must not be biased towards the irrelevance of the liquidity issues in the insurance sector, where cash flows are characterised in any case by a degree of uncertainty greater than that of other intermediaries. We must not ignore the fact that liquidity imbalances often prelude solvency crises, or that cash tensions often constitute their occurrence; this element alone should grant significance to the issue of maintaining conditions of adequate liquidity even in the case of insurance intermediaries.

We consider how recent developments in the market have led to a number of insurers being exposed to higher levels of liquidity risk. Such developments include (Bank of England/PRA 2019):

1. a move from some insurers to seek less liquid and potentially more volatile assets;
2. increased liquidity implications arising from reinsurance arrangements;
3. group funding arrangements;
4. increased use of derivatives in hedging, particularly with instruments that have mandatory central clearing.

Regardless of the sources of uncertainty attributable to the financial management, which are typical of any financial intermediary and identifiable in the difficulty to predict the degree of asset liquidity, the potential disposal conditions, as well as the variability of the current return deriving from the investments made, deviations in the performance of the expected incoming and outgoing cash flows in relation to the actuarial management may be attributable to the insurance undertakings' functional specialisation, especially with reference to the liabilities issued.

Liquidity tensions may originate from various factors, some of which are shared by life assurance and non-life insurance; others are specific to one or the other.

In the case of life assurance, in particular for savings policies, the liabilities present less uncertainty, since when the contract is stipulated the undertaking knows the extent of its obligation towards all policyholders, and not only towards some. Though in this case a better knowledge of the maximum liabilities amount can be tested, some elements of uncertainty do remain which assign the liquidity profile of the liability in relation to when the pure risk (risk of death or survival) occurs and any request to surrender the insurance savings plan (Kubitza et al. 2019).

As a matter of fact, we cannot ignore that the ever-greater opportunity granted to the insured parties to make use of the right to reduction or surrender of the policies increases the level of collectability of the liabilities issued in the life assurance. For example, the right to surrender, which, though discouraged at contractual clause level, constitutes a factor that reduces the availability of the provisions and, by subjecting the request for early settlement to the initiative of the insured, may generate financial imbalances.

Liquidity tensions may also arise from some technical characteristics of insurance management, or from deviations between estimated hypotheses and the real figures encountered.

In the first instance, we refer to the practice of paying the commissions for all premiums referring to the policy, including in the presence of periodic premium payments, to the agent at the time of stipulating the contract. This may generate significant liquidity tensions, especially in the lifelines, which are known for a particularly long contract duration.

Other technical causes may be attributed to the concentration in given periods of time of surrender requests (for life insurance) or to the irregularity of the distribution over time of claims (for life and non-life insurance).

Errors in the assessment of the extent of premiums—which is based exclusively on estimated or conjectured elements that vary in relation to the business lines considered—and, subsequently, of the size of the provisions, may also cause unexpected tensions for the liquidity situation. These errors are attributable to the difficulties in assessing the probability of occurrence of certain events and are proportionally more frequent in non-life insurance, where the construction of tables similar to the actuarial ones used in calculating life premiums is more complex and less reliable. This means that the premiums may not be sufficient to hedge the compensation paid to the insured parties exactly, underlining, even in this case, the correlation between actuarial risk and liquidity risk.

The technical bases used may prove to be inadequate due to deviations between the estimated and effective frequencies, as well as the deformation of the individual company's risk portfolio compared to the sector average; in this sense, the greater inconveniences regard small-sized undertakings, where it is more difficult to make the law of large numbers operate correctly.

The variability of cash flows may also be influenced by technical factors in the life unit, should the demographic hypotheses at the basis of the pure premium calculation be unexpected. Liquidity tensions could even be traced back to financial-equity management imbalances, in the event of considerable decreases in the effective return on the investments of the premiums set aside.

It must be added that deviations may also occur between estimated management costs and costs actually borne. This holds particular relevance in the lifelines, where by law it is necessary to estimate the acquisition, collection and management costs relating to the entire duration of the contracts in advance for the purposes of defining an average loading to be added to the pure premium. As mentioned previously, the acquisition commissions are paid fully to the agents when the contract is concluded, regardless of its outcome, whereas they are only recovered, based on the premiums, over time. Therefore, it is entirely normal for the costs actually incurred to deviate from those initially estimated due to the practical impossibility of making reliable predictions, over a particularly long time frame, regarding future business policies, as well as the predictable inflation and salary dynamics.

The adoption of integrated asset and liability management techniques through the construction of flow prediction models may also be proposed to tackle liquidity risk in insurance undertakings.

It is also clear that there is a need to improve liquidity management both through the formation of a securities portfolio with natural or negotiable liquidity on an efficient secondary market, and by using appropriate forms of debt or commitments recognised by lenders, through the transfer to third parties of the liquidity risk, such as techniques to reinsure the assumed risks.

2.4 *The Credit Risk Management*

Credit risk derives from the possibility that neither one of the parties to a contract will be able to satisfy, within the given times and methods, its financial obligation under that contract.

The Solvency II provisions define credit risk as "the risk of loss, or of adverse change in the financial situation, resulting from fluctuations in the credit standing of issuers of securities, counterparties and any debtors to which insurance and reinsurance undertakings are exposed, in the form of counterparty default risk, or spread risk, or market risk concentrations". Risk mitigation contracts are used as a reference, including reinsurance agreements, securitisation and derivatives, in addition to loans to intermediaries and any other exposure not hedged by the spread risk subcategory, with reference to the concept of Loss Given Default (LGD).

In light of the above, credit risk may be traced back to the different processes of insurance management, such as risk assumption processes, distribution processes, investment processes and reinsurance processes. An insurer, in particular, may be exposed to credit risk in the following areas:

1. Full or partial defaults by reinsurers, agents, brokers, other trade debtors and related parties such as policyholders;
2. Financial losses due to default or deterioration in credit quality (typically measured by a rating downgrade) arising from balances held with deposit-taking institutions, loan portfolios, securities issuers or investment counterparties.

In summary, the common credit risk mitigation measures may include policies and controls on:

- appropriate credit exposure limits to different types of approved counterparties. Such limits should take into account concentration risks to a group of related entities, economic sectors or geographical spread;
- credit criteria and analysis including the extent of reliance on ratings issued by external credit rating agencies;
- dealing with counterparties who no longer satisfy established criteria, e.g. pursuant to a trigger clause in a reinsurance agreement;
- approving, accepting and monitoring collateral, if any;
- ageing analysis of outstanding balances;

- monitoring the credit standing of debtors and counterparties;
- reporting credit exposures and any breaches.

Tackling credit risk therefore assumes the careful examination of the financial soundness of issuers of transferable securities, end borrowers of monetary resources and reinsurance undertakings using screening and monitoring techniques. This presupposes the selection of issuers with high levels of credit standing.

In policy-based and mortgage-back loans, credit risk may be contained by screening and monitoring, and, at the same time, by the existence of related guarantees.

Lastly, in reinsurance transactions, credit risk may also be reduced by selecting reinsurers with a high credit standing, by making use of their rating. In the phase following the establishment of the contractual relationship, the appropriate monitoring techniques are implemented, with which, as of rather recently, Alternative Risk Transfer (ART) operations are associated (Swiss Re 2000).

2.5 *The Operational Risk Management*

According to global regulatory authorities, operational risk is generally defined as "the risk of loss due to failed or inadequate internal processes, systems, people and external events" (BCBS 2006). The definition includes legal risk but excludes strategic and reputational risks. This also represents the basic definition for the measurement of operational risk, e.g. the calculation of required capital for operational risk under the Solvency II regime (Gatzert and Kolb 2014; Hampson and Ortega 2017).

Although insurers have largely adopted the same definition of operational risk used by other types of industries, it must be noted how the risk profiles of the insurance industries are different due to the complexity that distinguishes the nature of their business, which is reflected in the risk-taking of other entities or individuals (Epetimehin 2013; Torre-Enciso and Hernandez Barros 2013).

The different root causes of operational risk can be traced back to the following aspects (Karam 2014; Institute of Risk Management 2015):

1. *Internal processes*: failure in the design and execution of core insurance and support processes such as sales and marketing, underwriting, policy issuance, customer billing and premium collection, reinsurance placement, claims payments, actuarial reserving and outsourcing processes;
2. *Systems*: inadequate data and security protection, weak access checks, unstable and overly complex systems, lack of adequate testing prior to production and deficient systems/tools;
3. *People*: human error, fraud, unmanaged staff turnover, over-reliance on key personnel, skills insufficient for job requirements and inadequate management overview;
4. *External events*: natural disasters (floods, fires, earthquakes, etc.) as well as man-made disasters (terrorism, political and social unrest) may impact the ability to operate on an ongoing basis; changes in the regulatory environment including new regulations.

In this respect, the boundary insurance events that often stem from other risk events must not be ignored (insurance, market and credit), which are caused by operational failures by people, process, systems and/or external elements. Insurers are recommended to consider all boundary events when managing operational risk. A concrete example is the increase of costs following claims made by customers with a very high-risk profile due to errors in the underwriting process for a period of time.

Operational risk is increasingly important in the management and corporate governance of insurance companies. The attention that failure due to poor operational risk management has received in recent years is causing increasing concern in organisations regarding the importance of managing and controlling such risks, especially when changes in the economic, social and technological world are occurring more rapidly. Globalisation, technological developments, competitive environments and legislative requirements make the activities of insurance companies increasingly more complex.

Operational risk arises in the following circumstances:

- if not properly controlled, the increased use of highly automated technology can create risks arising from errors in manual data processing systems, due to the increased reliance on global integrated systems;

- the growth of e-business lending has a potential risk that is still not fully understood (e.g. internal and external fraud and system security issues);
- acquisitions and mergers, which make a large business difficult to manage;
- use of sophisticated products to manage financial risk.

Responsibility for the awareness and mitigation of operational risk lies with every employee. Usually, only a few individuals can expose insurance companies to extreme losses from insurance, financial, market or credit risk. In the case of operational risk, excessive exposure can be caused by any resource that the internal processes rely on (people, systems, infrastructure, etc.) (CRO Forum 2014).

To embed this risk awareness and culture it takes commitment from senior management, a strong and clear "tone at the top" and defined roles and responsibilities for the management team and employees in the business, risk management, independent assurance and audit functions. Moreover, it takes a robust framework that includes all elements ranging from identification, measurement and monitoring to control and mitigation activities, as well as business resilience and continuity processes (Buehler et al. 2019).

Incorporating operational risk management into all processes of the end-to-end value chain is a key element; because of this, it is important to involve senior management early in decision-making processes. The quality of the business and risk management processes drives the effectiveness of the operational risk management framework.

2.6 *The Legal and Compliance Risk Management*

Compliance risk is defined as the risk of incurring legal or regulatory sanctions, significant financial loss or damage to reputation resulting from the company's failure to comply with laws or regulations. This must not be confused with the legal risk that regards the risk of value loss or reduction of the portfolio assets due to underwriting inadequate or incorrect contracts or documents, or those containing clauses that prove to be particularly costly for the company. Legal risk must be understood as a manifestation of operational risk and regards aspects that we might define as formal.

The substantial aspect, on the other hand, takes precedence when we refer to compliance risk; here, non-compliance with the regulations must be considered in its operating, dynamic and concrete aspects. In fact, let us consider the circumstance for which undertakings normally have protections that—at least in intention—guarantee the operations' compliance with the regulations in force, particularly for transparency and fairness towards the insured, in terms of contractual and pre-contractual information, claims management, and in general, the protection of the policyholder-consumer. In practice, the same legislative evolution to protect policyholders leads to the consideration of the diverse, or substantial aspect; as a matter of fact, we know that in recent decades the constant evolution of the positive law has created new techniques to protect the weaker party that are no longer anchored in formal data, but aimed at recovering information symmetries and tangible contractual powers, driven also by the European legislator's incessant activity.

Therefore, the presence in the undertaking of adequate structures guaranteeing compliance with the legal regulations is a tool not only intended for internal efficiency, but also for an external profile, consistent in protecting the insured party.

When referring to compliance risk, we note how non-compliance with the laws leads to the deterioration of the company image as a possible consequence. It follows then that compliance risk may also generate a reputation risk.

In order to sustain a sound activity and guard against sanctions, insurers are required to identify and evaluate all non-compliance risks. The purpose of the identification and evaluation is to confine the residual risk to an acceptable level for the insurer. This policy requires the establishment of a risk map which shows non-compliance risks according to their probability of occurrence and level of importance.

This approach entails thorough knowledge of the company's strategic profile and of which goals to achieve in terms of risk management.

Compliance modernisation helps companies pursue their core mission and achieve compliance as efficiently and effectively as possible by thinking forward, then harnessing the best available compliance practices and technologies in order to comply with current and future regulatory requirements. This is an ongoing need driven by never-ending technological advancement and market expectations that are constantly on the rise. No matter how "modern" a company's existing compliance systems and processes might be, there is always room for improvement.

3 Conclusions

The continuously evolving complexity of the risk system accentuates the uncertain context in which the modern enterprise must operate.

The growing uncertainty is, therefore, the first point for comparison for the undertaking, in view of pursuing the primary purpose of value creation. Management must provide effective and fast responses to this uncertainty, evaluating first and foremost the maximum sustainable risk profiles, then adopting the subsequent measures to ensure the survival of the corporate body and satisfy stakeholders' expectations.

Following the financial crisis, the issue of risk governance in the financial sector rose to prominence. In this regard it has been stated that "the financial crisis can be to an important extent attributed to failures and weaknesses in corporate governance arrangements which did not serve their purpose to safeguard against excessive risk-taking in a number of financial companies" (Kirkpatrick 2009).

Though insurance companies were affected to a lesser extent by the financial crisis than banks, and their core business—risk undertaking—did not feel its effects, it has nevertheless been demonstrated that insurance companies with a stronger risk governance structure might be able to better control their shortfall risk (Magee et al. 2019).

It is also necessary to mention that risk management must not only be considered a defensive activity. During non-crisis periods, the purpose of risk governance is not to reduce risk per se, but to support appropriate risk-taking and increase the probability that a firm might achieve its business objectives (Stulz 2015).

References

Aebi, V., Sabato, G., & Schmid, M. (2012). Risk Management, Corporate Governance, and Bank Performance in the Financial Crisis. *Journal of Banking & Finance, 36,* 3213–3226.

Ai, J., Bajtelsmit, V., & Wang, T. (2018). The Combined Effect of Enterprise Risk Management and Diversification on Property and Casualty Insurer Performance. *The Journal of Risk and Insurance, 85*(2), 513–543.

Altuntas, M., Berry-Stölzle, T. R., & Hoyt, R. E. (2011). Implementation of Enterprise Risk Management: Evidence from the German Property-Liability Insurance Industry. *Geneva Papers on Risk and Insurance—Issues and Practice, 36,* 414–439.

Altuntas, M., Berry-Stölzle, T. R., & Hoyt, R. E. (2012). *Dynamic Determinants of Enterprise Risk Management Adoption* (Working Paper). University of Georgia.

A.M. Best Special Report. (2001, July). *AM Best's Enterprise Risk Model, A Holistic Approach to Measuring Capital Adequacy.*

Babbel, D. F., & Santomero, A. M. (1997). Financial Risk Management by Insurers: An Analysis of the Process. *The Journal of Risk and Insurance, 64,* 231–240.

Back, K., & Skipper, H. (1994). *Life Insurance.* Upper Saddle River, NJ: Prentice Hall.

Bank of England/PRA Prudential Regulation Authority. (2019, March). *Liquidity Risk Management for Insurers* (PS18/19/Consultation Paper 4/19).

Baxter, R., Bedard, J. C., Hoitash, R., & Yezegel, A. (2013). Enterprise Risk Management Program Quality: Determinants, Value Relevance, and the Financial Crisis. *Contemporary Accounting Research, 30*(4), 1264–1295.

BCBS—Basel Committee on Banking and Supervision. (2006). *Basel II: International Convergence of Capital Measurement and Capital Standards: A Revised Framework.* Comprehensive Version.

Beasley, M. S., Branson, B., & Hancock, B. (2009). *Report on the Current State of Enterprise Risk Oversight.* Raleigh: ERM Initiative at North Carolina State University.

Beasley, M. S., Clune, R., & Hermanson, D. R. (2005). Enterprise Risk Management: An Empirical Analysis of Factors Associated with the Extent of Implementation. *Journal of Accounting and Public Policy, 24,* 521–531.

Berry-Stölzle, T. R., & Xu, J. (2018). Enterprise Risk Management and the Cost of Capital. *The Journal of Risk and Insurance, 85*(1), 159–201.

Bohnert, A., Gatzerta, N., Hoytb, R. E., & Lechnera, P. (2019). The Drivers and Value of Enterprise Risk Management: Evidence from ERM Ratings. *The European Journal of Finance, 25*(3), 234–255.

Buehler, K., Carpineti, M., Kerjan, E. M., Nauck, F., & Serino, L. (2019, November). The Value for Insurers in Better Management of Nonfinancial Risk. *McKinsey on Risk,* no. 9.

Colquitt, L. L., Hoyt, R. E., & Lee, R. B. (1999). Integrated Risk Management and the Role of the Risk Manager. *Risk Management and Insurance Review, 2,* 43–61.

CoSO—Committee of Sponsoring Organizations. (1992). *Internal Control—Integrated Framework.*

CoSO—Committee of Sponsoring Organizations. (2004). *Enterprise Risk Management—Integrated Framework: Executive Summary and Framework.*

CoSO—Committee of Sponsoring Organizations. (2013). *Internal Control—Integrated Framework.*

CoSO—Committee of Sponsoring Organizations. (2017). *Enterprise Risk Management—Integrating with Strategy and Performance.*

CRO Forum. (2014). *Principles of Operational Risk Management and Measurement.* Available at http://www.thecroforum.org.

Cumming, C. M., & Hirtle, B. J. (2001). The Challenges of Risk Management in Diversified Financial Companies. *FRBNY Economic Policy Review, 7,* 1–17.

Daly, R., & Kapel, A. (2006). *Market Risk—Life Insurers Compared to Banks.* Financial Services Forum. Sydney: Institute of Actuaries of Australia.

De Finetti, B., & Emanuelli, F. (1967). *Economia delle assicurazioni.* Turin: Utet.

Dickinson, G. (2001). Enterprise Risk Management: Its Origins and Conceptual Foundation. *The Geneva Papers on Risk and Insurance—Issues and Practice, 26*(3), 360–366.

Eckles, D. L., Hoyt, R. E., & Miller, S. M. (2014). The Impact of Enterprise Risk Management on the Marginal Cost of Reducing Risk: Evidence from the Insurance Industry. *Journal of Banking & Finance, 43,* 247–261.

Epetimehin, F. (2013). Managing the Impact of Operational Risk on the Solvency of Insurance Companies. *OIDA International Journal of Sustainable Development, 5*(12), 69–78.

Farrell, M., & Gallagher, R. (2015). The Valuation Implications of Enterprise Risk Management Maturity. *The Journal of Risk and Insurance, 82*(3), 625–657.

Floreani, A. (2005). *Introduzione al Risk Management. Un approccio integrato alla gestione dei rischi aziendali.* Milan: Etas.

FSB—Financial Stability Board. (2013). *Thematic Review on Risk Governance.* www.financialstabilityboard.org.

Gardner, M. J., & Mills, D. L. (1988). *Managing Financial Institutions: An Asset/Liability Approach.* Chicago: Dryden.

Gatzert, N., & Kolb, A. (2014). Risk Measurement and Management of Operational Risk in Insurance Companies from an Enterprise Perspective. *The Journal of Risk and Insurance, 81*(3), 683–708.

Gatzert, N., & Wesker, H. (2012). A Comparative Assessment of Basel II/III and Solvency II. *The Geneva Papers on Risk and Insurance—Issues and Practice, 37,* 539–570.

Grace, M. F., Leverty, J. T., Phillips, R. D., & Shimpi, P. (2015). The Value of Investing in Enterprise Risk Management. *The Journal of Risk and Insurance, 82*(2), 289–316.

Hampson, C., & Ortega, G. (2017). *The Fundamentals of Operational Risk for Insurers.* London: Risk Books.

Hoyt, R. E., & Liebenberg, A. P. (2011). The Value of Enterprise Risk Management. *The Journal of Risk and Insurance, 78*(4), 795–822.

Institute of Risk Management. (2015). *Operational Risk Modelling: Common Practices and Future Development.* London: Internal Model Industry Forum.

Karam, E. (2014). *Measuring and Managing Operational Risk in the Insurance and Banking Sectors*. Business Administration. Lyon: Université Claude Bernard.

Kirkpatrick, G. (2009). The Corporate Governance Lessons from the Financial Crisis. *OECD Journal: Financial Market Trends, 1*, 61–87.

Kleffner, A. E., Lee, R. B., & McGannon, B. (2003). The Effect of Corporate Governance on the Use of Enterprise Risk Management: Evidence from Canada. *Risk Management and Insurance Review, 6*, 53–73.

Kubitza, C., Berdin, E., & Gründl, H. (2019, March). *Rising Interest Rates and Liquidity Risk in the Life Insurance Sector* (ICIR Working Paper Series No. 29/17).

Lam, J. (2001). The CRO Is Here to Stay. *Risk Management, 48*, 16–20.

Lechner, P., & Gatzert, N. (2018). Determinants and Value of Enterprise Risk Management: Empirical Evidence from Germany. *European Journal of Finances, 24*(10), 867–887.

Liebenberg, A. P., & Hoyt, R. E. (2003). The Determinants of Enterprise Risk Management: Evidence from the Appointment of Chief Risk Officers. *Risk Management and Insurance Review, 6*(1), 37–52.

Magee, S., Schilling, C., & Sheedy, E. (2019). Risk Governance in the Insurance Sector—Determinants and Consequences in an International Sample. *The Journal of Risk and Insurance, 86*(2), 381–413.

Marrison, C. I. (2002). *The Fundamentals of Risk Measurement*. New York: McGraw-Hill.

McShane, M. K., Cox, L. A., & Butler, R. J. (2010). Regulatory Competition and Forbearance: Evidence from the Life Insurance Industry. *Journal of Banking & Finance, 34*, 522–532.

McShane, M. K., Nair, A., & Rustambekov, E. (2011). Does Enterprise Risk Management Increase Firm Value? *Journal of Accounting, Auditing & Finance, 26*(4), 641–658.

Meulbroek, L. K. (2002). Integrated Risk Management for the Firm: A Senior Manager's Guide. *Journal of Applied Corporate Finance, 14*, 56–70.

Nair, A., Rustambekov, E., McShance, M., & Fainshmidt, S. (2014). Enterprise Risk Management as a Dynamic Capability: A Test of Its Effectiveness During a Crisis. *Managerial and Decision Economics, 35*, 555–566.

Nocco, B. W., & Stulz, R. M. (2006). Enterprise Risk Management: Theory and Practice. *Journal of Applied Corporate Finance, 18*(4), 8–20.

Pagach, D., & Warr, R. (2011). The Characteristics of Firms That Hire Chief Risk Officers. *The Journal of Risk and Insurance, 78*(1), 185–211.

Poufinas, T., & Tsitsika, P. (2018). An Assessment of the Market Risk Solvency Capital Requirement Simplifications for Insurance Undertakings. *Theoretical Economics Letters, 8*, 2363–2387.

S&P—Standard & Poor's. (2005). *Criteria, Insurance, General: Evaluating the Enterprise Risk Management Practices of Insurance Companies*. www.standardandpoors.com.

S&P—Standard & Poor's. (2013, May). *Criteria. Insurance. General: Enterprise Risk Management.*

Stulz, R. M. (2015). Risk-Taking and Risk Management by Banks. *Journal of Applied Corporate Finance, 27*(1), 8–18.

Swiss Re. (2000). *L'asset-liability management per le compagnie di assicurazione*. Sigma 6.

Torre-Enciso, M. I., & Hernandez Barros, R. (2013). Operational Risk Management for Insurers. *International Business Research, 6*(1), 1–11.

CHAPTER 4

Risk Governance in the Second Pillar of Solvency II Framework

Abstract The chapter focuses on the prudential supervisory provisions ensuing from the second pillar of Solvency II. Starting from the assumption that simple quantitative measures are not always sufficient to identify and appropriately define the undertaking solvency profile, the second pillar establishes qualitative requirements to address risks not specifically mitigated by the solvency capital requirements. The chapter, after focusing on the main provisions on corporate governance, also analyses how Solvency II encourages insurance undertakings to adopt a global approach in order to strengthen the processes of corporate risk governance and to systematise the key four functions: risk management, compliance, actuarial and audit function which bolster the "three lines of defence" structure in the system of risk governance.

Keywords Solvency II · Corporate governance · Risk governance · Risk management function · Own risk and solvency assessment · Compliance function · Actuarial function · Internal audit function

1 Introduction

In the intentions of the Solvency II regulatory framework, the culture of risk—which also belongs to the history of the insurance industry since its origins—becomes the real business engine (European Commission 2007).

A. Cappiello, *The European Insurance Industry*,
https://doi.org/10.1007/978-3-030-43142-6_4

This, therefore, clarifies that one of the objectives of the overall design of Solvency II is to discern all the quantitative capital requirements and other qualitative elements of corporate management—including the supervisory process—that might influence the company's solvency situation in terms of risk. The second pillar of Solvency II, that deals, as already stated, with the qualitative requirements of the new prudential system, is expressly designed for this purpose (Eling et al. 2007; Buckham et al. 2010; Andenas et al. 2017; Rae et al. 2018). At a glance, the fundamental assumptions of the regulatory approach may be summarised as follows:

a) the quantitative regulation does not in any case allow for the adequate identification and definition of the risks that impact the insurance business. With reference to this, it must be mentioned that the first pillar of Solvency II, in addition to setting out the general principles and the quantitative regulations relating to technical provisions and investments, aims to quantify the capital protections against underwriting, market, credit and operational risks, leaving room, if necessary, for the adoption of internal models. The second pillar targets the qualitative assessment of the risks that cannot be quantified in the first pillar;
b) for the purposes of a risk-based prudential supervisory system, the implementation of internal control and risk management systems is fundamental. In this, we can certainly see the intention to move undertakings towards an appropriate and advanced application of reporting, assessment and management techniques and the related monitoring of corporate risk;
c) lastly, the intention to standardise and create coordination between authorities, tools and supervisory practices with a view to European integration—and material unification—of the market and undertakings is by no means secondary.

BOX 1—Second Pillar: qualitative requirements

- Greater role of the Board in risk management.
- Qualitative risk management standards referring to all risks, not only to those hedged by first-pillar quantitative requirements.

- Requirements on tasks and responsibilities of key control functions: risk management, actuarial function, compliance and internal audit.
- Prospective assessment of company and group risks (ORSA) and subsequent assessment of the medium- to long-term overall solvency requirement.
- Reporting to the supervisory authority.
- Possibility of increased capital requirement (*capital add-ons*) following the supervisors' assessment (e.g. if the *standard formula* does not reflect the undertaking's real risk profile due to significant shortcomings in the corporate governance system in risk management).

2 Main Provisions on Corporate Governance of Insurance Undertakings

The principles and regulations around which the dynamics of coordination and control of the powers and tasks within the undertaking are built gives, as a whole, consistency to the concept of corporate governance (OECD 2015; Tylecote and Visintin 2008; Huse 2007; Calderini et al. 2003; Roe 2003).

Nevertheless, the operating conditions of the entire business in terms of efficacy, efficiency and competitiveness are greatly influenced by the relationships between individuals and related interests, specifically when and how these are disentangled in certain structures of equity investment in the capital of the company.

The goal of a valid corporate governance system is to support the process of creating and distributing value by virtue of a governance and control system that protects the interest of stakeholders through a managerial action characterised by effective strategy, information transparency and managerial correctness (Hopt 2013; Ricci 2014; Brogi 2008).

In recent decades the authorities of all jurisdictions have profoundly, and in detail, amended the prudential rules for the entire financial and insurance system, with interventions intended to increase the capital requirements on the one hand, and to change the governance rules of companies on the other. The recognition of the importance of good governance practices was fundamental to the development of Solvency II framework, which states "some risks may only be properly addressed through governance requirements rather than through the quantitative requirements reflected in the Solvency Capital Requirement. An effective system of governance is therefore essential for the adequate management of the insurance undertaking and for the regulatory system" (whereas no. 29, Solvency II Directive).

Insurance sector regulation and supervision have played a key role in shaping the corporate governance of insurers; indeed, the regulatory framework is often a key determinant of governance standards within insurers (European Commission 2010; EIOPA 2015a; Boubakri 2011).

As a matter of fact, awareness of the importance held by an efficient corporate governance system drives insurance companies to keep their system constantly in line, not only with continuous legislative changes but also with national and international best practices. This is all explicitly recognised by law in Solvency II, which brought numerous innovative elements, in particular impacting profoundly on the dynamic assessment of insurance company risks, and on their management models (Kleffner et al. 2003; Financial Stability Board 2014; IAIS 2017).

Under Solvency II, each insurance company must have an effective governance system in place to provide for the sound and prudent management of its business. Good governance rules, which are industry neutral, are joined by specific elements for the insurance sector, such as the structures and processes of the risk control system (Dell'Atti and Sylos Labini 2019).

Governance requirements have generally been designed to improve the quality and independence of decision-making, to promote sound risk management and internal control policies and procedures, and to promote proper transparency, reporting and disclosure, thereby helping to reduce the incidence of default, promote market discipline and protect the interests of policyholders as well as any third parties that may have direct claims against an insurer under an insurance agreement (Siri 2017).

Of the innovative aspects introduced by Solvency II, the verticalisation of decision-making processes must not be forgotten, as it leads to a greater accountability of the executive management team. In particular, the role of the Board of Directors (the Board) is reinforced, whose necessary prerequisite resides in elevated professional competence and stringent requirements of honesty, integrity and competence in order to provide sound and prudent management.

Solvency II is engaged, first of all, in affirming the central role of the Board in the overall governance system of the undertaking. The Board's centrality manifests across a series of new tasks and responsibilities assigned to it and in the strengthening of functions that have always been under its responsibility (Besher and Furusten 2018; Dell'Atti et al. 2018).

Among other things, key duties and responsibilities of the Board include:

- obtaining reassurance that a framework of prudent and effective controls is in place which enables risk to be assessed and managed throughout the company;
- supporting the development of the company's strategy having due regard to the overall strategy of the company and being satisfied that the agreed strategy is appropriately executed;
- reviewing, challenging and approving the Own Risk and Solvency Assessment (ORSA) process;
- ensuring the integrity of financial information and that the financial controls are robust and defensible;
- overseeing the company's processes and framework to ensure compliance with its regulatory and legal obligations.

The Solvency II requirements on the system of governance are aimed at providing for sound and prudent management of the undertakings' business without imposing a predefined organisational structure, as long as they establish an appropriate segregation of duties.

Nevertheless, the regulator provides that at least the key four functions must be included in the system of governance, namely the risk management, the compliance, the actuarial and the internal audit function, which bolster the "three lines of defence" structure in the system of risk governance.

3 The Four Key Functions in the System of Risk Governance

In the insurance industry, the regulation and supervision of the internal governance system have a fundamental role within the risk management framework, since some risks may only be correctly tackled using governance requirements (Venuti and Alfiero 2016; Marano and Siri 2017; Magee et al. 2019).

Within the governance system, the second pillar confirms the central role of control activities structured across the following four functions—all pertaining to the end responsibility of the Board—where "function" is defined as the internal capacity to undertake practical tasks and does not necessarily mean a specific person or department (art. 13, par. 29, Solvency II directive):

- Risk management function
- Compliance function
- Internal audit function
- Actuarial function

In turn, the functions have to satisfy a range of requirements, such as fulfilling the "fit and proper" requirements, complying with certain reporting requirements and being in a position to perform their tasks and exercise the authorities given to them. The functions must be able to fulfil their responsibilities objectively, fairly and independently; so, for example, the internal audit function may only be performed by an independent unit.

The establishment of the four key functions for Solvency II bolsters the "three lines of defence" structure of the risk governance system.

The first line, related to the front-line operational units, is responsible for the identification, analysis, assessment and management of risks on a day-to-day basis.

The risk management, actuarial and compliance functions form the second line, monitoring and managing all of the risks at aggregate level and controlling the underwriting guidelines and approvals in the operational units.

As the third line of defence, internal audit is responsible for the performance of internal controls; it regularly reviews the entire governance system and all other activities in the company.

3.1 The Risk Management Function

According to article 44 of the Solvency II Directive, the risk management function, alongside the organisational structure and decision-making processes, must be structured in such a way as to facilitate the implementation of the risk management system, which includes strategies, processes and reporting procedures necessary to continuously identify, measure, monitor, manage and report current and potential risks and their interdependencies at an individual and aggregate level.

The risk management function operates in complexity, since Solvency II interprets the function as a relevant driver of the decision-making process. As a matter of fact, with Solvency II the risk management function plays a key role in the company's strategic planning, by coordinating the process to define the risk appetite and providing preventive indications useful to the senior management in order to guarantee the alignment and adequate level of integration between risk management, the business model and strategic planning.

Risk management policies define the risk categories, from a current and prospective standpoint, and the methods used to measure said risks. Specifically, they cover all risks, quantifiable or otherwise, including strategic and reputational risks where relevant.

The risk management function is responsible for producing correct guidelines for the development of strategies and processes for identifying, measuring, monitoring, managing and reporting risks within a company. It is also responsible for calculating the solvency capital requirements, the agreement and management of the risk profile, the appropriate consideration of interactions between different risk categories and the identification and systematic integration of emerging risks.

At a minimum, the risk management system should cover the following areas: risk assumption and reserving; asset/liability management; investments, especially derivatives; management of liquidity and concentration risks; management of operational risks; reinsurance, and other risk mitigation techniques.

In addition to coordinating the overarching risk management activities, this function must also identify potential risks and recommend appropriate countermeasures to the Board. The ORSA, including from a prospective standpoint, indeed represents one of the main new developments imposed by the current prudential supervisory regime.

It is also shown how the risk management function, while performing its activities, must in specific circumstances cooperate with the actuarial function (art. 48, Solvency II Directive). In addition to the abovementioned "fit and proper" requirements, the risk management function will no doubt have to include individuals with a professional, scientific and mathematical background, ideally backed by appropriate qualifications (e.g. actuaries).

The risk management function also has reporting responsibilities: relevant risks must be represented qualitatively and quantitatively, as well as internally and externally. The function must report to the Board on the effectiveness of and any shortcomings in the risk management system, and on the ORSA results (e.g. the development of risk capital in the coming years).

If a company uses an internal model or partial model to calculate its risk capital requirements, the risk management function has significant additional responsibilities including the design, implementation and validation of the internal model, which are joined by the reporting tasks to the Board about the performance of the internal model, suggesting areas in need of improvement, and updating said body on the status of efforts to improve weaknesses identified previously.

3.1.1 The Own Risk and Solvency Assessment Process

Solvency II requires that, in the context of its risk management system, each insurance undertaking must perform an own ORSA by evaluating the risks to which it is exposed, including future risks.

The ORSA can be defined as "the entirety of the processes and procedures employed to identify, assess, monitor, manage, and report the short- and long-term risks a (re)insurance undertaking faces or may face and to determine the own funds necessary to ensure that the undertaking's overall solvency needs are met at all times" (CEIOPS 2008).

Specifically, the overall solvency needs assessment covers all material risks, including unquantifiable risks such as reputational or strategic risk, which are not, however, included in the SCR calculation (EIOPA 2015b, 2017). The process must at least involve the overall solvency needs, taking into account the specific risk profile, approved risk tolerance limits and the business strategy of the undertaking; continuous compliance with the capital requirements and the requirements for technical provisions imposed by the regulator; the extent to which the undertaking has deviated from the hypotheses underlying the solvency capital requirement.

Therefore, the ORSA, as required by law, must adopt a "forward-looking perspective", taking into consideration any risk to which it could be exposed in future with a reasonable level of probability. These risks may derive from internal factors, such as amendments or additions to the company's business plan, or from external factors.

BOX 2—The Solvency II ORSA Process
Risk Assessment

☐ Consider link between risk profile, approved risk tolerance limits and overall solvency needs
☐ Identify material risks
☐ Assess current risks against risk appetite
☐ Assess risks not quantified in the Solvency Capital Requirement standard formula calculation
☐ Assess future risk profile in line with future business plans.

Generate SCR using standard formula

☐ Elicit data from systems
☐ Validate input
☐ Consider expert judgement
☐ Second set of eyes reviews and ultimately calculate SCR and Minimum Capital Requirement.

Execute Technical Provisions

☐ Execute the technical provisions process to calculate technical provisions for the company in compliance with relevant articles and for input for the standard formula calculation.

Validate

☐ Validate data at all stages. Include second set of eyes reviews where appropriate.

Capital and Solvency Review

☐ Consider appropriateness of SCR standard formula given current risks faced
☐ Internally assess economic capital needs for the current year and over the medium term based on the company's strategy
☐ Assess available funds against capital requirements (both current and projected).

Stress and Scenario Testing

☐ Annually assess risk, capital and solvency position under stress conditions

☐ Stress tests determined annually by risk management function.

Documentation

☐ Produce a record of each ORSA/Internal ORSA Report
☐ All documentation to support and facilitate completion of online ORSA reporting tool.

As part of the forward-looking assessment of own risks (FLOAR), companies must perform regular stress tests, reverse stress tests and scenario analyses.

Stress tests are used to assess the impact on the financial situation of unfavourable trends of the risk factors, considered individually or combined into a single scenario (Lavelle et al. 2010; Clarke and Phelan 2015).

Stress tests must provide prognostic hypotheses in relation to the maximum losses that could occur in given scenarios or hypotheses. These scenarios, which generally predict three levels of possible economic outcomes—best case, middle case and worst case—in which each of the key factors, such as interest rates, returns and liabilities evolve in the best possible way, normally or in the worst way imaginable, provide different levels of premises to create a hypothetical outcome that allows for an adequate risk assessment.

Reverse stress tests, on the other hand, calculate the level of stress for individual risk factors capable of reducing the solvency ratio below a pre-established minimum threshold, such as the risk appetite.

Lastly, the scenario analyses measure the effect on the prospective solvency profile of changes in the economic/financial context which are reflected in the simultaneous change in several risk factors.

For the purposes of the ORSA, the company develops its process in consideration of the nature, scope and complexity of the risks pertaining to the business according to the principle of proportionality; this principle is not exclusively reflected in the level of complexity of the method used, but also in the frequency with which the ORSA process is implemented.

The results of the assessment process, performed at least annually and approved by the Board, are communicated to the supervisory authorities and internally to the control bodies and business units involved (EIOPA 2015b).

The ORSA process makes it possible for the risk and solvency assessment to be an integral part of the company strategy, so as to guarantee a constant alignment between strategic planning and risk management.

Specifically, the strategies defined by companies to manage their solvency needs and the capital requirements imposed by the regulation must be perfectly integrated with the methods of managing all risks to which the undertaking is exposed. For these very reasons, the ORSA, as a part of the risk management process, must be considered a fundamental process that drives business management and, in particular, the strategic business decisions and management processes (EIOPA 2015b).

The regulation therefore requires strong integration of the ORSA process in strategic decisions. In particular, the ORSA must be applied by companies as a strategic planning management tool as well as a tool to measure company strategy effectiveness.

Furthermore, the ORSA—when performed efficiently and communicated clearly—can improve the basic information for Board decisions and increase the undertaking's credibility towards supervisors, as well as it can contribute to anticipate the company's future risks and direct the strategic planning process.

EIOPA published a supervisory statement that outlined the first supervisory experiences on how European (re)insurance companies have implemented the ORSA process (EIOPA 2017). This statement is based on the supervisory assessments of ORSA under the Solvency II framework and utilises the information collected by the national supervisory authorities in the European Economic Area (EEA) following Solvency II implementation in 2016.

The analysis shows that the majority of (re)insurance companies made good progress in implementing the ORSA process; however, according to EIOPA, further improvements are needed. Analysis indicates that Board members must play a more active role in the ORSA process—they must take greater consideration of the results of these assessments in their decision-making processes. It also indicates the over-reliance of insurers on the standard formula with regard to risk management. Therefore, to properly determine the overall solvency needs of companies, EIOPA stressed the importance of thoroughly assessing any significant deviations in company risk profiles from the standard formula. The quality of stress test scenarios used in the ORSA process needs to be further improved and the risk assessment needs to cover the impact of all potential risks.

3.2 The Compliance Function

Compliance with regulations is a fundamental aim in order to protect the objective of creating value and increasing stakeholder confidence.

The compliance function is responsible for assessing the adequacy of procedures, processes and the internal organisation, with the aim of preventing non-compliance risk, defined as the risk of incurring penalties, financial losses or reputation or image damages deriving from the violation of external provisions (laws, regulations and instructions from supervisory authorities) and internal provisions (e.g. articles of association, codes of conduct, internal disciplinary codes).

The compliance function established within companies must be in proportion to the nature, extent and complexity of the risks arising from the business activities.

To provide early warning of problems, the compliance function must consider possible future changes in the legal environment and their potential effect on the company. This also includes the "compliance plan" to be produced by the compliance function, mentioned in Guideline 41 of the framework Directive, which should cover as a minimum the compliance risk and the risk of legal changes for the following financial year (Baxter 2014; Dreher 2015).

Any violation of the law at a company must be investigated and followed up by the compliance function and reported to the Board, and in certain circumstances to external bodies such as the financial supervisory authority.

In particular, the compliance function must: continuously identify the laws applicable to the undertaking and assess their impact on business procedures and processes; assess the adequacy and effectiveness of the organisational measures adopted to prevent risk and non-compliance with the law and propose the organisational and procedural amendments intended to ensure adequate organisational risk monitoring; assess the effectiveness of the organisational adjustments subsequent to the suggested amendments; and prepare adequate information flows for the company's corporate bodies and other structures involved. Furthermore, other duties of the compliance function concern: the setting up of a specific organisational unit; the appointment of the function manager; the annual presentation of an activity programme; the preparation of a report to the Board regarding the adequacy of the monitoring adopted (Limentani and Tresoldi 2014; Tarullo 2014).

The organisational placement of the compliance function is left at the undertakings' discretion, albeit in respect of the principle of segregation between operational and control functions. Particularly, companies can establish the function in the form of a specific organisational unit, or, taking into account the nature and reach of the risks pertaining to the business, through the use of resources belonging to external units (Elderfield 2012).

It is also important to highlight the close links between compliance, risk management and internal audit functions, explicitly defined and formalised by the administrative body. This said, the compliance function is separate from the internal audit function in the sense that the former is subject to periodic checks by the latter.

3.3 The Actuarial Function

Given the unique nature of the insurance industry, alongside the functions mentioned previously, an effective actuarial function is also envisaged.

This function, particularly complex, has a wide range of responsibilities, which can be broken down into three core areas:

- Coordination and monitoring of the evaluation of technical provisions, including methodology, assumptions and data;
- Reporting;
- Supporting the risk management function.

Within the actuarial function there must be a clear separation of responsibilities and appropriate controls for the evaluation of the technical provisions. The function is not responsible for calculating the technical provisions, but for coordinating the calculation process and assessing the methods, tools and data used for the evaluation. One of the main tasks of the function is to coordinate and monitor the appropriateness of the methodologies and models used to calculate the technical provisions (Lloyd's of London 2012; Williams et al. 2015).

Due to the types of tasks to be performed by the actuarial function, it is likely that it will have to provide considerable support to the risk management function by supplying actuarial expertise. In particular, it will be necessary for it to help with the calculation and modelling of the underwriting risks and contribute actuarial methodology to the calculation of capital (own funds) and risk capital requirements. This function is also required to give its opinion on the effectiveness of reinsurance cover. This may concern a number of areas. In addition to the effect of reinsurance on risk capital, diversification and the economic balance sheet, it is also important to assess the expected development of business and the ensuing need for reinsurance cover in the following years (AAE 2016).

Where internal models are used, the function is required to perform in-depth analyses of and express its views on their design and use. In this area in particular, it needs to work closely with the risk management function to ensure consistency between reserving and calculating the risk capital requirement.

It is also necessary for the actuarial and risk management functions to work together on certain parts of the ORSA, especially the confirmation that the technical provisions have been calculated in accordance with the Solvency II requirements.

In the reporting area, the actuarial function is required to communicate regularly with the Board and advise other units on technical provisions.

It must submit an annual report to the Board essentially covering the results of the above-mentioned activities. On the basis of this report, the Board should be in a position to form an opinion on the appropriateness of the technical provisions calculation, the underwriting guidelines and the reinsurance guideline. The report should also provide detailed explanations of changes in the assumptions and the reasons for the changes (best estimates compared to experience values).

An assessment of the reserving, the underwriting policy and the reinsurance cover as well as the interaction between them is also required. Possible weaknesses and deficiencies in all the areas mentioned must also be reported, with recommendations for rectification. Deficiencies may be due to a lack of expertise or specialist knowledge (e.g. in the case of new and complex products).

Considering the responsibilities of the actuarial function, it is clear that in addition to satisfying the "fit and proper" requirements, its staff must have in-depth actuarial and mathematical knowledge. Companies must ensure that the actuarial function is able to perform its tasks objectively, appropriately and independently. This means, for example, that there must be a clear separation of responsibility for calculating the technical provisions and monitoring said calculation, with different reporting lines.

3.4 *The Internal Audit Function*

The internal audit function, which constitutes the third of the three lines of defence, is one of the characteristic elements of the internal controls system framework, as well as a fundamental function of the governance system (IIA 2009; Sosnowski et al. 2015).

In contrast to the other key functions, internal audit is an independent function that is not permitted to undertake operational tasks nor the tasks of other key functions.

Solvency II requests that companies perform audits with a risk-based arrangement of the activity that extends to the evaluation of all elements of the governance system. Specifically, the prudential supervisory regime requires that companies arrange the auditing activities according to the notion of ongoing management.

The internal audit function is defined as an independent, objective assurance and consulting activity whose role is to add value, improve an organisation's operations and ensure the respect of regulatory obligations. It helps an undertaking to accomplish its objectives by providing a systematic, disciplined approach to evaluate and improve the effectiveness of risk management, the actuarial function, the compliance function and internal governance processes, thereby helping them protect the assets, reputation and future sustainability of the organisation (Chartered Institute of Internal Auditors 2013).

Therefore, the areas to be examined by the internal audit function concern:

- Effectiveness and efficiency of processes and controls.
- Compliance with rules, instructions and requirements relating to risk controls and operational capability (including reliability, accuracy and completeness).
- Timing and frequency of reports (including external reporting).
- Availability and reliability of IT systems.

The internal audit function fulfils its role by assessing whether the significant risks of the organisation are appropriately identified; assessing whether those risks are mitigated appropriately and assessing whether the organisation operates in an efficient and effective manner (see Chapter 6).

In principle, all of a company's activities are subject to internal audit. The internal audit function must nevertheless plan the activities to identify which priority areas require an audit, including in relation to the costs and available resources.

Assuming the internal audit function operates effectively means that the internal audit function is expected to design and implement an audit plan that encompasses the whole internal audit scope (activities, components and functions) as amended by the Solvency II framework.

Internal audit should prepare an audit plan based on its own risk assessment of the entire governance system and ensure that all significant activities are audited at appropriate intervals. Internal audit may well request that other units provide reports or opinions on the internal controls to be performed. The actual performance of the audits and the assessments given are the sole responsibility of the function itself, which must act on its own initiative and not be subject to external influence. The function is permitted to advise other units on controls to be performed provided that giving this advice does not jeopardise its independence (ECIIA Insurance Committee 2019).

The resultant findings and recommendations, which derive from auditing activities, must be the subject of reports. The internal audit function must conduct its audits and communicate its findings in an entirely objective manner, and not be subject to any instructions from any other department or function. The independence and impartiality of internal audit must be guaranteed. The audit report, to be produced at least annually, should contain information on internal audit's achievement of its objectives and the degree of completion of the audit plan. Internal audit should report possible shortcomings and recommend remedial action with deadlines for completion, specifying the persons responsible. The function should also monitor the rectification of the shortcomings.

Since the internal audit function is responsible for reviewing all parts of the governance system and hence the other key functions, it is difficult to provide a clear definition of the "fit and proper" requirements. All internal audit engagements must be performed with proficiency and due professional care. This means that internal auditors must have or must acquire, where necessary, the knowledge, skills and any other competences needed to perform their individual responsibilities (Global Institute of Internal Auditors 2017). However, due professional care does not imply infallibility and, in some cases, the internal audit function should legitimately consider the support of an external expert in the subject, in order to ensure an adequate level of expertise on specific areas to be covered according to the internal audit plan.

4 Conclusions

An effective control system must guarantee a close interconnection with all other variables present within the company system such as organisational, individual, technical and social variables. This system must present a clear distribution and appropriate separation of responsibilities, in addition to making it possible to transmit information effectively (Ernst & Young 2018).

In this regard, it is evident that there may be some overlaps between the four key functions mentioned above. It will then be the Board's responsibility to define, document and communicate clear segregation of duties. The internal control and risk management system directives, approved by the Board, define, among other things, the interactions between the key functions in order to render their operations more effective and efficient. These interactions determine coordination in the planning of activities, continuous exchange of information, common taxonomies, processes, instruments and methodologies for risk assessment.

In order to guarantee the effectiveness of the governance system, the key functions ought to work in close synergy, and there should be a regular exchange of information.

For example, via the internal control system, the compliance function has a preventive role in avoiding violations and following up any potential infringements, while the risk management function is responsible for analysing and assessing the compliance risk and taking it into account in the overall risk profile and risk management process.

On the other hand, the interfaces between the risk management and actuarial functions are numerous, and concern the close collaboration necessary to guarantee, for example, consistency of methodology and models for the calculation of the risk capital requirement or in calculations performed for the ORSA.

This said, the three functions, risk management, actuarial and audit are expected to provide opinions on underwriting activities with different focuses. The risk management function analyses the impact on the company's overall risk situation; the actuarial function considers in particular the interdependencies between the underwriting policies and the implications for reserving; internal audit verifies the operational capacity and effectiveness of the internal control system with reference to the decision-making and evaluation processes.

Lastly, both the internal audit and risk management functions are responsible for monitoring the operational effectiveness of the risk management system and identifying potential risks at an early stage. Monitoring by the risk management function is directed primarily at the operational units in the first line of defence, while internal audit is concerned with both the first and second lines, the latter including the risk management function itself.

References

AAE—Actuarial Association of Europe. (2016, June). *The Role of Actuaries Under Solvency II*. Brussels: AAE.

Andenas, M., Avesani, R. G., Manes, P., Vella, F., & Wood, P. R. (2017). *Solvency II: A Dynamic Challenge for the Insurance Market*. Bologna: Il Mulino.

Baxter, T. C. (2014, July 23). *Reflections on the New Compliance Landscape*. New York: Federal Reserve Bank.

Besher, A. R., & Furusten, S. (2018). New International Rules for Corporate Governance and the Roles of Management and Boards of Directors. In S. Alexius & S. Furusten (Eds.), *Managing Hybrid Organizations: Governance, Professionalism and Regulation* (pp. 321–332). Cham: Palgrave Macmillan.

Boubakri, N. (2011). Corporate Governance and Issues from the Insurance Industry. *Journal of Risk and Insurance, 78*(3), 501.

Brogi M. (2008). *Corporate governance e sistema dualistico per banche e assicurazioni*. Carefin WP, 3/08, 1–65.

Buckham, D., Wahl, J., Munagala, S., & Rose, S. (2010). *Executive's Guide to Solvency II*. Hoboken, NJ: Wiley.

Calderini, M., Garrone, P., & Sobrero, M. (Eds.). (2003). *Corporate Governance, Market Structure and Innovation*. Northampton and Cheltenham: Edward Elgar.

CEIOPS. (2008, May). Issue Paper 27.

Chartered Institute of Internal Auditors. (2013). *Guidance on Effective Internal Audit in the Financial Service Sector*. Available at: https://www.iia.org.uk/resources/sector-specific-standards-guidance/financial-services/financial-services-code/.

Clarke, S., & Phelan, E. (2015). *Stepping Stones to ORSA: Looking Beyond the Preparatory Phase of Solvency II* (Milliman Research Report). Available at: http://www.milliman.com/.

Dell'Atti, S., & Sylos Labini, S. (2019). *Il governo societario nelle imprese di assicurazione. Regolamentazione, proporzionalità e gestione del cambiamento*. Milan: Wolters Kluwer.

Dell'Atti, S., Sylos Labini, S., & di Biase, P. (2018). The Effects of Solvency II on Corporate Boards: A Survey on Italian Insurance Companies. *Corporate Ownership & Control, 16*(1–1), 134–144.

Dreher, M. (2015). *Treatises on Solvency II*. Berlin: Springer-Verlag.

ECIIA Insurance Committee. (2019, June). *Internal Audit in the Insurance Industry Guidance.*

EIOPA. (2015a, January). *Guidelines on System of Governance*. Frankfurt.

EIOPA. (2015b, January). *Guidelines on Own Risk and Solvency Assessment.* Frankfurt.

EIOPA. (2017, June). *Supervisory Assessment of the Own Risk and Solvency Assessment—First Experiences* (Eiopa-BoS/17-97). Frankfurt.

Elderfield, M. (2012, December). *Effective Enforcement—Encouraging Compliance and Good Practice.* Opening remarks to the Central Bank Enforcement Conference, Dublin.

Eling, M., Schmeiser, H., & Schmit, J. T. (2007). The Solvency II Process: Overview and Critical Analysis. *Risk Management and Insurance Review, 10*(1), 69–85.

Ernst & Young. (2018). *Internal Audit in Insurance—Current Market Issues and Trends.* Available at: https://www.ey.com/Publication/vwLUAssets/EY-internal-audit-in-insurance/$FILE/EY-internal-audit-in-insurance.pdf.

European Commission. (2007, July). *Proposal for a Directive of the European Parliament and of the Council on the Taking-Up and Pursuit of the Business of Insurance and Reinsurance.* Solvency II, Brussels.

European Commission. (2010). *Corporate Governance in Financial Institutions and Remuneration Policies* (Green Paper). Available at: http://ec.europa.eu/internal_market/.

Financial Stability Board. (2014, April). *Guidance on Supervisory Interaction with Financial Institutions on Risk Culture.* Available at: http://www.fsb.org/.

Global Institute of Internal Auditors. (2017, January). *International Standards for the Professional Practice of Internal Auditing.* Lake Mary, FL: The Institute of Internal Auditors.

Hopt, K. J. (2013). *Better Governance of Financial Institutions* (EGGI Law Working Paper 207/2013).

Huse, M. (2007). *Boards, Governance and Value Creation: The Human Side of Corporate Governance.* Cambridge: Cambridge University Press.

IAIS—International Association of Insurance Supervisors. (2017, March). *Insurance Core Principles, Standards, Guidance and Assessment Methodology.*

Kleffner, A. E., Lee, R. B., & McGannon, B. (2003). The Effect of Corporate Governance on the Use of Enterprise Risk Management: Evidence from Canada. *Risk Management and Insurance Review, 6,* 53–73.

Lavelle, D., O'Donnel, A., Pender, D., Roberts, D., & Tulloch, D. (2010, November). *The Solvency II ORSA Process.* Society of Actuaries in Ireland.

Limentani, R. N., & Tresoldi, N. (2014). *Compliance Handbook*. Rome: Bancaria Editrice.

Lloyd's of London. (2012). *Solvency II Guidance on the Report of the Actuarial Function*. Available at: http://www.lloyds.com/~/media/Files/The%20Market/Operating%20at%20Lloyds/Solvency%%20Guidance_Final%20v2.pdf.

Magee, S., Schilling, C., & Sheedy, E. (2019). Risk Governance in the Insurance Sector—Determinants and Consequences in an International Sample. *The Journal of Risk and Insurance, 86*(2), 381–413.

Marano, P., & Siri, M. (Eds.). (2017). *Insurance Regulation in the European Union: Solvency II and Beyond* (pp. 129–177). Cham: Palgrave Macmillan.

OECD. (2015). *Principles of Corporate Governance*. Available at: http://www.oecd.org.

Rae, R. A., Barrett, A., Brooks, D., Chotai, M. A., Pelkiewicz, A. J., & Wang, C. (2018). A Review of Solvency II: Has It Met Its Objectives? *British Actuarial Journal, 23*(4), 1–72.

Ricci, O. (2014). *Corporate Governance in the European Insurance Industry*. Berlin: Springer.

Roe, M. J. (2003). *Political Determinants of Corporate Governance: Political Context, Corporate Impact*. Oxford: Oxford University Press.

Siri, M. (2017). *Corporate Governance of Insurance Firms After Solvency II* (ICIR Working Paper Series No. 27), 1–39.

Sosnowski, J., Bardon, L., & Guez, D. (2015). *Positioning the Internal Audit Function Within the Solvency II Framework*. Deloitte. Available at: https://www2.deloitte.com/.

Tarullo, D. K. (2014, October 20), *Good Compliance, Not Mere Compliance, at the Federal Reserve Bank of New York Conference: Reforming Culture and Behavior in the Financial Services Industry*. New York.

The Institute of Internal Auditors—IIA. (2009). *The Role of Internal Auditing in Enterprise-Wide Risk Management*. Lake Mary, FL: IIA.

Tylecote, A., & Visintin, F. (2008). *Corporate Governance, Finance and the Technological Advantage of Nations*. London and New York: Routledge.

Venuti, F., & Alfiero, S. (2016). The Impact of Corporate Governance on Risk Taking in European Insurance Industry. *World Academy of Science, Engineering and Technology, 10*(1), 188–194.

Williams, R. L., Anzsar, J., Bulmer, R., Buntine, J., Byrne, M., Gedalla, B., et al. (2015). *Application of the Solvency II Actuarial Function to General Insurance Firms, Actuarial Function Working Party, Institute and Faculty of Actuaries*. Available at: https://www.actuaries.org.uk/system/files/field/document/Actuarial%20Function%20Working%20Party%20paper.pdf.

CHAPTER 5

The Evolving Risk Landscape: Impact on Internal Control and External Regulation

Abstract The insurance sector, along with the rest of the financial sector, has faced significant changes in recent years, and such changes have brought new products and services, new tools, new styles of competition and new risks. Following an analysis of the main megatrends that impact the insurance industry, the chapter focuses on new control challenges to better cope with the evolving scenario, where insurance activities become ever riskier and more complex. Furthermore, the chapter focusses on the impact of these potential changes on external regulation and on the revision of the existing regulatory regime.

Keywords Insurance trends · Insurance competitive scenario · Financial convergence · InsurTech · Insurance value chain · Solvency II revision

1 Introduction

In the early years, many trends had a major impact on the insurance sector. A variety of technological, cultural and economic developments modifies the nature of risks, open doors to new entrants, drive convergence of sectors and create new ecosystems.

The risks that need to be insured are changing significantly for two primary reasons. First, uncertainty will be reduced as tracking and predictive technology improves. For example, connected cars have fewer accidents

A. Cappiello, *The European Insurance Industry*,
https://doi.org/10.1007/978-3-030-43142-6_5

and breakdowns, predictive maintenance reduces business interruptions, and wearables help ensure a healthier lifestyle. Second, substantial changes in risk distribution and actuarial models (for example, due to an increasing number of long-tail risks) are further aggravating this trend. A resulting demutualisation could shift the focus to predicting and managing the risks of individuals rather than communities.

As a consequence, premiums can be expected to come under pressure, reducing what have traditionally been rather stable revenue streams. Insurers have to look over their business models with a holistic view of the developments and the opportunities that could offer new revenue sources.

2 Trends in the Insurance and Financial Sector: New Competitive Landscape

At both European and global level, the insurance and financial sector has experienced contemporary megatrends (as defined by Naisbitt 1982), which at a social, economic, political and technological level have produced profound structural change in recent decades. One key factor in these developments has been the banking and insurance sectors simultaneously competing and cooperating with one another.

Financial convergence takes on a competitive character whenever an insurance company/bank offers a product that has similar characteristics to a banking/insurance product. An alternative financial convergence method consists in forming a new company in the adjacent sector (insurance/banking) or acquiring a company already active in that sector (Slepov et al. 2019; Voutilainen and Koskinen 2019).

On the other hand, alliances have been formed between banks and insurance companies. The benefit of this arrangement is the increased potential for effective cross-selling and diversification of business portfolios. This means that banking offers also envisage insurance products, and, at the same time, insurance offers also consider banking products. A bank can cross-sell life insurance, for example, to its deposit and mortgage customers, and non-life insurance to almost any customer of another service. The drawbacks include high capital costs and often discontinuity in the business results.

The most preferred alliance model from executive management's point of view is a financial conglomerate—banks and insurance companies operating under common ownership.

A financial conglomerate is an entity composed of a parent company, at least one bank and at least one insurance company. The parent company can be a holding, a bank or an insurance company. The benefits to this model include better customer relations management, easier construction of the profits approach, better product development management, more efficient sales channels management where conflicts between them are overcome, and the diversification of the business portfolio.

There is also expansion beyond the financial sector, with banks and insurance companies that begin joint operations in other fields. At the same time, non-financial companies have entered the insurance and financial sector.

Customer relations management and the often complicated IT systems associated with it can be managed more efficiently when the relevant parties belong to the same group of companies. Success is influenced considerably by the power balance of the parties involved and the distribution of responsibilities. Simplification of the profit approach (i.e. distribution of profits via commission) is made more possible when one party in the alliance has authority over the other. Product development is also more streamlined when one party is superior to the other in terms of authority. A merger often results in a reduction of worker numbers. This is more easily dealt with if one party is clearly subordinate.

The diversification of the business portfolio is an undeniable priority in large groups. Profits and losses are evened out when the conglomerate's combination of banking and insurance functions involves bank and non-life insurance operations. Conversely, bank and life insurance activities amplify profits and losses. Therefore, banking and the non-life insurance are a better fit for one another in terms of portfolio diversification (Estrella 2001).

Lately, banks and insurance companies have experimented with a new type of convergence and competition deriving from retail chains. Financial convergence has therefore taken another step forward, transforming into industrial convergence, where non-financial industries penetrate the banking and insurance sectors while financial firms enter new business areas.

In more recent years, the growing diffusion of advanced technologies has led to further evolution in the competitive dynamics with the entry onto the market of InsurTech start-ups. InsurTech identifies all technology-driven innovation in the insurance industry: software, applications, start-ups, products and services. The InsurTech sector is demonstrating the same dynamic in the insurance sector as that which affected the entire financial service industry, with the creation and spread of start-ups that use technology to innovate one or more steps of the traditional financial institution's value chain (Mackenzie 2015; Baumann 2018; Behm et al. 2019).

Most InsurTech investments are concentrated in innovation in the non-life compartment, particularly in the health and motor segments. However, diversification by area is growing and though investments were primarily concentrated in marketing and distribution, which are still predominant, they now extend to solutions in the field of analytics and underwriting on demand, namely the specific activity of selection and risk assessment of policies sold to policyholders. The trend is to intervene in all phases of the insurance value chain and even in different insurance sectors than the non-life compartment (Braun and Schreiber 2017; Deloitte 2018b).

All stages of the customer's journey and the value chain may be affected by the InsurTech phenomenon. As a matter of fact, the digital innovation macro-trend is leading to a much more fluid state in the sector, where each value proposition can become the integration of a set of multiple modules belonging to different players. At the same time, the boundaries are increasingly blurred between the classic roles of distributor, supplier (at times from another sector), insurer and reinsurer. In this scenario, the balance of power is questioned, and consequently, as is the share of the profit pool pertaining to the various participants. Each one can cooperate or compete according to the context and moment.

The context seems to favour further growth of InsurTech, despite the high level of regulation in the insurance sector (Capgemini and Efma 2019). Conversely, the very presence of entry barriers hinders access to the market by global digital giants such as Google, Facebook and Amazon. Without players in a strongly dominant position, the sector has the chance to develop gradually and widely, giving InsurTech the time and room to manoeuvre to gather funding and develop new solutions.

InsurTech start-ups generally adopt very linear business models focussed on specific areas and rich in technological content almost entirely dedicated to innovation in the insurance sector. Most use artificial intelligence, specifically machine learning, and possess a great capacity for Big Data analysis and processing. Due to their significant digitisation, these start-ups are able to seize the opportunities offered by the market more swiftly than traditional companies. As such, they often have a culture that strives for and honours innovation and a mentality that places them in pole position in sector change.

In the early stages of their market entry, the innovative business model of InsurTech start-ups raised concerns about whether they would constitute a threat to the incumbent companies, due to a process named "digital disruption".

However, the difficulties that a start-up might encounter are manifold, so some tech-led initiatives in insurance will inevitably fail. Factors of disadvantage are due to poor market knowledge, the lack of an appropriate business model as well as the high level of competition in the insurance sector, characterised by many complexities and a high level of technical content.

Though new players generally have strong skills in terms of customer experience, simplification and process speed, traditional companies have a significant advantage over the competitors entering the sector, namely the considerable reputation they enjoy on the market and a huge pool of information about customers in terms of biographical data and, above all, risk profiling. In addition, the size of incumbent companies, with their conspicuous capital structures and the possibility to access new resources fairly easily, enables them to enter new market sectors, improve their services, support the launch of new products and attempt risky strategies (Cappiello 2018).

Moreover, recent surveys report that customers do not seem ready to abandon traditional insurance providers, as they consider them to be more reliable in terms of security and protection against fraud, attributing great value to brand reputation and personal interaction.

It follows that InsurTech and BigTech do not pose an immediate competitive threat to established insurers. A drastic disintermediation of insurance companies, which would also imply a profound innovation of the incumbent business models, does not seem to lie ahead in the short-to-medium term.

Insurance companies are beginning to perceive new start-ups not as market disrupters, but rather as potential partners, just as traditional banks and FinTech did, where they began working closely together to offer the best possible customer experience to their customer base, both in the relationship stage, carried out by the incumbent companies, and in the management of the "customer-centric" approach, executed by the innovators (Vanderlinden et al. 2018).

To improve their products and customer service and limit the damage deriving from the arrival of new entrants, insurance companies have started signing partnership agreements with InsurTech start-ups in order to build profitable partnerships with new operators and, on the other hand, to safeguard and possibly increase their market share. These initiatives bear witness to the fact that incumbent operators are beginning to understand the potential of the InsurTech sector and to consider the digitisation of their business model as a positive thing.

An increasing number of insurers now regard investment in digitisation as a priority, especially considering that the sector has lagged behind its financial services peers in adopting digital technologies owing to regulations, reluctance and cost.

Many incumbent insurers are seeking to upgrade their digital capabilities, especially in order to boost customer engagement and collect data about new risk pools. In some cases, insurers have increased spending on research and development to foster in-house innovation. Some are working with BigTech, while other insurers are investing directly in and/or partnering with start-ups. Furthermore, the majority of entrants also seem willing to adopt a collaborative strategy with the incumbent companies.

The development of alliances with new competitors (such as InsurTech suppliers) allows the incumbents to take advantage of the expertise, dynamics and ways of doing business, which, by its very nature, the insurance industry could not have developed alone. Big Data analytics and Blockchain projects are now the most interesting developing areas in the medium term for the insurance sector.

Technology and new data sources are fundamentally changing our economy and society, and promise to transform the insurance industry as well. New technology start-up firms—or InsurTech—are entering the industry to deliver some of the services typically provided by incumbent insurers and intermediaries. Industrial companies as well as established technology firms are eyeing up opportunities in insurance. The new entrants present opportunities for mutually beneficial partnerships with insurers but they could also become direct competitors, putting pressure on profit margins and challenging the insurers, especially at customer interface.

3 Digital Transformation of the Insurance Value Chain

Similarly to banks, insurance companies have been very slow in adapting to digitisation and in taking advantage of the opportunities offered by digital transformation. However, the now unrestrainable digitisation process is greatly affecting all activities that make up the insurance chain and forcing radical changes upon corporate culture, products and processes, data management, customer relations and relations with the sector's various competitors (Eling and Lehmann 2018).

We can identify three change areas produced by:

1. Technologies which allow for automation, standardisation and improvement of the efficiency of productive processes as regards, for example, online sales, the management of policy offers and claims management;
2. Technologies which are able to modernise existing products or create new ones, as they allow for the possibility to generate more accurate risk pools thanks to increased market understanding;
3. Technologies which modify the interaction between insurers and policyholders thanks to the development of distribution methods that introduce alternative contact methods between customers and insurers that meet customer needs based on service complexity.

It follows that technological innovation revolutionises the entire insurance business to a great extent, since it plays an incisive role in every area of activity.

Big Data, artificial intelligence/cognitive computing, predictive modelling, telematics and the Internet of Things (IoT) are having an impact all along the insurance value chain, leading to the automation of business processes (e.g. automated processing of contracts, automated reporting of claims) and decisions (e.g. automated underwriting, claim settlement, product offerings, asset and risk management) (OECD 2017a; Schmidt 2018).

Product development mainly avails itself of Big Data analytics, which is combined with the use of IoT—systems of interrelated sensors/devices—and Blockchain ledgers which allow for the development of "smart contracts" that are capable of executing or enforcing themselves in the complete absence of human intervention.

The collection and analysis of Big Data facilitate knowledge of potential customers and the identification of their risk profile. They improve the competitiveness of the products and services offered by adapting offer personalisation to customers' needs in terms of quality and price.

The ability to collect and use Big Data proves crucial in order to analyse the vast quantity of information, structured and unstructured, arising from telematics devices, social networks and other sources (customer feedback, etc.). Machine learning algorithms are developed in order to improve the quality of data analysis to be used for customer segmentation and risk allocation.

IoT could revolutionise product design by opening up many new opportunities in connected home and health solutions. Among IoT systems, we find wearable devices, i.e. smart objects able to monitor policyholders' state of health in real time, thus allowing them to receive customised offers and respond promptly to sudden illnesses and for companies to check customers' habits. Cheap, connected monitoring devices offer a fundamentally different way of assessing and, crucially, mitigating risk, thus also reducing the rate of fraud through a constant monitoring of risk positions.

Technological progress also makes it possible to underwrite risk which could not have been insured until now since new technologies are able to reduce the problem of information asymmetries thanks to refined risk-level calculations, as adopted by companies on the basis of the interpretation of the insured party's data. The data are collected using intelligent sensors and devices and allow for more precise identification of the insured risks. In this regard, IoT/Big Data Analytics Technologies open the door to new ways of assessing and managing risk and claims.

Risk selection is becoming ever more accurate and precise. The ways in which technology is improving or will improve risk selection include: (i) the use of data gathered from connected sensors (IoT); (ii) the use of Big Data to enrich underwriting decisions; (iii) forward-looking, sophisticated risk measurement (catastrophe modelling); and (iv) digitalisation of insurance, which makes data more readily analysed and products more readily adapted.

The growing proliferation of new data about insured parties collected via sensors and smart devices allows for a more granular underwriting and monitoring of individual risks. Software solutions recognise patterns in the data and cluster them, giving insurance companies more detailed insight into the behaviour and needs of their customers.

Thanks to the use of telematics and wearable technologies, it is possible to gather some parameters in real time during the entire policy life cycle, such as driving behaviours and the health metrics of insured parties.

The combination of rich customer data, telematics and enhanced computing power makes it possible to adopt premiums based on the actual use and conduct of the insured. Insurers can use the real-time data captured through telematics devices and powerful analytics to reassess the current risks and recalculate the premium for current risks at regular intervals. Insurers can develop tailor-made products with pricing adjusted to individual risk levels and a very accurate selection.

Companies with innovative pricing models and information about individual risks can better identify the lowest-risk customers, while self-informed, higher risk customers may seek out less sophisticated providers offering more attractive rates based on less information. In this environment, late adopters of new technology would be more susceptible to the threat of adverse selection.

The opportunity to collect and analyse in real time a wide variety of data is transforming claims processes, enabling insurers to improve fraud detection, cut loss-adjustment costs, and eliminate many human interactions. Artificial Intelligence and Big Data are the main instruments to adopt in order to carry out claims management correctly: thanks to the sophisticated analysis, it is possible to prevent false accident fraud, automate claims calculation and manage their payment (Balasubramanian et al. 2018; Albrecher et al. 2019).

Sales and distribution are undoubtedly the value chain components which have been affected most by the technological evolution. The interdependence between production, distribution and consumption phases makes the delivery system decisive in the connotation of the service, as well as in its qualification with the customer. The application of digital technologies has vastly changed the service delivery process, the way they are used and, consequently, the customer relationship. In this regard, we must observe how the technological variable should be managed by the company not only from a purely productive perspective (to streamline procedures and reduce operating costs), but also in terms of marketing to improve the corporate image.

It is essential to underline how the digital evolution poses new challenges and issues for the insurance industry. In this respect, reference is made to the increasing competition between insurance companies, due, among other things, to the frequent overlapping of areas of expertise made possible by the growing spread of technologies.

The loss of direct contact with the customer is undoubtedly a negative factor that must not be overlooked. It is therefore necessary to balance the need for a personalised relationship with customers with the benefits offered by automation. This objective can be achieved by seeking a pronounced standardisation of elementary services, which must be associated with a greater specialisation of the company–customer relationship.

Lastly, it cannot be disregarded that is not an easy task to adopt technologically advanced solutions in a sector as strongly regulated and historically imposed as the insurance sector, where stringent regulation and consolidated governance slow innovation.

Furthermore, the use of big data raises legal and ethical questions. Debate is rife around the unconditional use by insurers of all data collected for decision-making purposes, as well as around how much time they might hold on to data, and which actions must be taken to protect these data from possible piracy attacks (EIOPA 2019a).

4 New Control and Regulatory Issues in Light of Emerging Risks

In recent decades the insurance industry has faced serious challenges. Operators and investors in mature markets have been hit hard by the low-interest-rate environment. Rising globalisation increased risk in insurance and finance, since all hedge funds, banks, brokers/dealers and insurance companies are highly interrelated (Billio et al. 2012). This is likely increasing the level of systemic risk in the finance and insurance industries through a complex network of relationships that changes on multiple time scales (Mendoza and Quadrini 2010). New digital new entrants (including aggregators) are reshaping the competitive landscape and altering the cost curve (Swiss Re Institute 2017).

Emerging risks, from cybersecurity to the increasing frequency and severity of natural catastrophes, also threaten to destabilise undertakings' strategies.

The use of new technologies has created a greater understanding of customer data and insight for strategy formulation on services and product development (Catlin et al. 2018). However, current digital developments also open the door to new vulnerabilities (EY 2017).

In this regard, cyber risk is gaining such relevance that it constitutes one of the main sources of operational risk faced by organisations, with it being considered the top risk in many countries (CRO Forum 2018, 2019; Egan et al. 2019; Buehler et al. 2019).

The increasing frequency and sophistication of cyber attacks, the fast digital transformation and the increased use of big data and cloud computing make insurers increasingly susceptible to cyber threats. Insurance companies also form a natural target for cyber attacks, as they possess substantial amounts of confidential policyholder information. In contrast to other sectors, which mainly hold sensitive financial data, insurers typically also collect a large amount of protected sensitive personal information. Data created through digitisation are invariably at risk of being hacked, accessed by criminals, lost or exposed to unauthorised users, both internally and externally.

The main consequences suffered by insurers following cyber incidents are business interruption and material costs for policyholders and third parties. In addition to the direct financial consequences, cyber incidents may also lead to serious and long-term problems for the insurance companies involved, since reputation damage can be substantial and even entirely irreversible.

The management of cyber risks entails numerous processes including the identification, analysis and measurement of potential effects in the context of cyber incidents. Furthermore, the need to implement preventive measures and consolidated action plans in order to face potential cyber incidents is crucial for building a more resilient system.

A study by EIOPA (2019a) highlights that the industry is aware of the potential cyber threats and has incorporated cyber risk explicitly in its risk management framework. Nevertheless, further actions are needed to strengthen the insurance sector's resilience against cyber vulnerabilities, in particular considering the dynamic nature of cyber threats. This would include streamlining the cyber incident reporting frameworks across the insurance and financial sector to avoid inconsistencies in the reported information and ultimately enhance operational resilience.

Of the crisis management mechanisms applied to the digital context, proposals have been developed to launch institutional reforms in order to make products, services and processes more secure and harmonised throughout Europe. The implementation of the Directive on security of network and information systems (NIS Directive) and the General Data Protection Regulation (GDPR) are two of the key initiatives in this regard

(EY 2017). It is necessary to create a sound cyber resilience framework for insurers. Harmonised general requirements on cyber security governance as part of operational resilience would help ensure the safe provision of insurance services (Keller 2018).

Lastly, we must consider how other risks such as environmental, social and governance (ESG) risks are becoming more significant in insurance (WEF 2018).

Weather events driven by climate change, social pressures as a greater legislative focus on treating customers fairly and governance issues that potentially lead to significant fees or reputation damage, may compromise the financial capacity of insurers.

ESG risks, which cover a series of factors related to the sustainability and social impact of the insurers' activities and their risk profiles, are not new to the insurance industry, but have become a strategic focus for many global insurers since knowledge and access to information about the main sustainability trends is increasing between regulatory authorities, investors and consumers (UNEP 2019).

ESG risks, like any other risk, may compromise the creditworthiness of insurers. For example, the credit profile of an insurer could be negatively influenced by an excessively concentrated exposure to catastrophe risks, which are amplified by climate change.

The three ESG risk categories involve insurers in different ways. For instance, property and casualty (P&C) insurers are significantly more exposed to environmental risks than life insurers, which in turn tend to be more exposed to social risks such as an ageing population.

It may be considered that governance risks affect insurers of all kinds more or less equally, even if larger insurers, which must comply with multiple jurisdictions, face a more complex series of governance challenges.

In some cases, the emergence of an ESG risk could give rise to another. For example, an environmental risk such as an increase in the frequency or severity of weather events, could increase the costs of (re)insuring catastrophe risks. This could become a social problem if as a result the insurance premiums were to become unaffordable for homeowners (The Geneva Association 2018).

Sustainable finance is modelling the behaviour of insurers. The insurance industry controls and manages a significant portion of global investable assets, while at the same time providing risk transfer capabilities (UNEP 2009; OECD 2017b; EIOPA 2018a). This puts insurers at the forefront of the movement towards sustainable finance, defined by the European Commission as "the provision of finance for investments that take into account environmental, social and governance considerations. It also exposes them to public and regulatory scrutiny" (European Commission 2019a).

In many parts of the world, insurers, as main investors, are subject to growing pressures from policymakers, supervisory authorities and customers so that they perform a full role in allocating capital in the development of a sustainable economy.

A number of international developments have accelerated the shift towards sustainable finance, including the Paris Climate Agreement (December 2015), the United Nations 2030 Agenda for Sustainable Development (September 2015) and the European Commission Action Plan on Sustainable Finance (March 2018).

Insurers are implementing a series of measures both in terms of investments and in terms of insurance risk, driven by their own assessment of the threats and opportunities linked to ESG risks, and by the need to respond to external pressures (Bacani et al. 2015).

The move towards sustainable financing is made complicated by the nature of some ESG risks, such as climate change, and by the uncertainty associated with their evolution over time. In addition, insurers must tackle the complex task of balancing their obligations towards various stakeholders, including policyholders, shareholders and society in general.

What has been discussed briefly thus far outlines how the fast changes to the insurance industry require a continuous improvement to the already sophisticated levels of internal control and existing risk management techniques and approaches.

It is clear that as the global economy grows, the need for different risk management approach will be necessary. Due to these challenges, the majority of insurance companies are changing their business models to address emerging insurance market challenges and to maintain their relevance in a competitive business environment (OECD 2019).

However, the new technologies that can expose organisations to risks can also be used to address these risks. These innovations are also impacting common control procedures, the overall control environment, risk management and auditing. There is no doubt that technology can enhance the quality, rigour and efficiency of internal controls. Organisations must consider how to embed technology into the control framework in a safe way, while taking into consideration the risks that arise with the use of technology.

Internal control concepts and principles, such as those in CoSO's Internal Control Integrated Framework (CoSO 1992), will continue to be applicable and relevant in the digital age. Indeed, technology can make internal controls even more effective, efficient and pervasive (Pwc 2019).

Many organisations are already deploying or exploring emerging technologies for control tasks or processes. In the future, we expect these technologies to be used more widely for control purposes (Grima 2019).

In the digital age, data governance and control culture will become more important as more controls become embedded in automated systems. Beyond this, a level of professional scepticism must remain to challenge the systems and be able to identify when the system could be wrong. The CFO and finance function play a key role in both embedding a data-driven control culture and maintaining a sceptical mindset.

Continuous testing and monitoring of controls requires interdisciplinary teams and skill sets of audit specialists (to test controls), business process owners (to oversee their processes) and technical staff (to build the technology-enabled control systems).

In this respect, we see the importance of a sound risk culture within an insurance organisation that needs to support the long-term goals effectively, and in particular the risk vision that a company has set (CRO Forum 2015).

Although risk culture is often associated with the elimination or minimisation of risk, we argue that it is crucial that it supports the desired level of risk-taking, driven by and aligned to the risk vision. It is necessary to consider the risk culture as an integral part of an overall risk management framework. A company can make use of sophisticated risk management tools, models, processes and functions, but if its risk culture is not aligned with the objectives set, these tools, models and processes cannot operate successfully.

4.1 Towards a Review of the Existing Regulatory Solvency II Regime

Undoubtedly, the Solvency II Directive framework has called upon insurance undertakings to operate in a context with connotations of greater integration, transparency, stability and competitive equality in the transnational market, created by aligning the quantitative regulatory requirements and the economic cost of risks faced by the company. The current regulatory system does allow for a homogeneous identification of the risks to which insurers are exposed, equipping them with effective tools to monitor their overall exposure through the identification and quantification of the risks associated with different sectors, the investment and credit positions assumed and the effects of risk diversification and transfer. In this way, the false incentives to assume positions for which there are no appropriately onerous capital requirements are eliminated. On the other hand, stakeholders benefit from the prudential protection of invested capital, which would impact (i.e. reduce) the probability of incurring losses. This then increases market confidence, bringing about virtuous processes where Solvency II moves towards an improvement in regulation and supervision, risk management, pricing calibrated on the effective risk underwritten.

These undoubtedly positive aspects are nevertheless countered by certain limits that diminish the structural and implementing potential of Solvency II. In addition, the megatrends that we have discussed briefly in previous pages also require renewed regulatory regimes (Schmautz 2016; Rae et al. 2018, Marullo 2018).

With the recent conclusion of an initial review of Solvency II in 2018, a second review is now on the way, this time more radical. This is an important opportunity to remedy the weaknesses of the European prudential supervisory regime, without underestimating the difficulties this review will face.

It seems appropriate, then, to summarise the main gaps that emerged in the initial years of Solvency II application, in the awareness that the consequences of the planning errors will likely continue to be felt even after the long-awaited reform.

The result of multiple compromises, over time Solvency II has clarified various limitations, both general (excessive complexity, scarce application of the proportionality principle, procyclical nature of the measures) and technical and detailed (prudential treatment of equity investments, inefficiency of anti-cyclical measures such as the *volatility adjustment*, treatment of government bonds).

One general critique emerges in relation to the gradual loss of the initial principle-based arrangement in favour of an excessively prescriptive system, created with the purpose of limiting the discretion of the supervised parties. Where complexity goes to impact transparency, simplification objectives should lead a review towards the much sought-after balance between prudent requirements on the one hand, and simplicity and clarity on the other.

Some gaps may even be found in the scarce application of the proportionality principle with respect to the nature, scope and complexity of the risks pertaining to the insurance or reinsurance activity of smaller undertakings.

Furthermore, we must not neglect the possibility that the Solvency II regulations may have a distorting impact on the investment strategies of insurance undertakings.

In this regard, it is considered that equity securities, given the higher volatility, are subject to a higher capital requirement than fixed income assets. It follows that companies, with policies to rebalance their portfolios, may decide to acquire greater volumes of low-risk fixed income instead of equity securities, considering that the latter's potentially higher return does not offset the cost of higher capital requirements.

Solvency II does not encourage shareholding, with the result that the quota of securities destined for investments in the life business remains low in insurance balance sheets. At a time when the economy is threatened by the risk of stagnation, equity investments perform an important role in creating long-term wealth and can offer an effective response in a context of very low interest rates. From this point of view, the European Commission project to introduce some benefits in favour of a new class of shares held in the long term is certainly interesting. However, it may prove to be inefficient if, as it currently seems, the proposal is subject to complex and restrictive conditions that may limit the expected effect on the long-term financing of the European economies.

Other more detailed aspects have also been the subject of criticism from the very beginning. These include the procyclical nature of the capital requirement calculation, since own funds cannot act as a buffer for shocks, while, on the contrary, they are destined to grow in difficult periods.

Though acceptable in principle, the approach to evaluating the assets and liabilities at market value, with the subsequent solvency capital requirement (SCR) calculation, has exposed the prudential indicators to short-term fluctuations in the financial markets, rendering them artificially volatile and rather incoherent with the business model (EIOPA 2019b).

This also occurs in the presence of *long-term guarantees* (LTGs)—including the *volatility adjustment* (VA)—, conventional mechanisms designed to mitigate the market value principle, given the exceptional short-term volatility that the financial markets may experience (EIOPA 2019c). The aim is to allow insurers to continue offering products with long-term guarantees.

Nevertheless, the annual reports by the EIOPA clearly demonstrate that, although these measures have been widely used throughout Europe, they have had a rather variable impact on the solvency situation depending on the country in which they are applied. The current conception and calibration of LTG measures may not function as desired, pushing insurers to deviate from adequate/optimal ALM strategies, and to create "distorted" investment strategies in Europe, with potential effects on said market volatility (Richard 2016; EIOPA 2017, 2018b).

The partial volatility adjustment review performed in 2018, though useful in the short term, does not tackle in a structural manner the functioning problems at the basis of the mechanism created to counter artificial volatility. A wider reform of said measure in favour of long-term investments and to protect the real economy from the effects of an excessive volatility must be faced in the review process of the Solvency II directive, which is scheduled for completion at the end of 2020 (Deloitte 2018a).

Lastly, it is considered that Solvency II, by encouraging an explicit modelling of the risks and their correlations, identifies the importance of diversification as a fundamental component in risk management (CRO Forum 2005).

Undertakings that effectively resort to diversification or belong to an insurance group should then have lower capital requirements than isolated and/or less diversified parties. Even if this effect is in line with the economic principles underlying the proposal, and does not decrease the level of protection offered to policyholders, it could nevertheless encourage the concentration trend already seen in the European insurance market, with a subsequent increase in the competitive pressure already exercised on small- and medium-sized insurance undertakings.

However, to tone down the consequences of this observation, we must consider that many small-sized companies are specialised insurers that monitor and carefully manage their risks and that are particularly favoured by their proximity to their customers, the relative simplicity of the product structure and the lower complexity of the assets portfolio. In these cases, these natural competitive advantages are recognised and may still translate in practice to a reduction in the cost of solvency requirements.

5 Conclusions

The Solvency II review process, officially launched with the Call for Advice sent by the European Commission to the EIOPA in February 2019 and which is to be complete at the end of 2020 (EIOPA 2019b, d), follows an approach of evolution rather than revolution of the pre-existing framework, where the fundamental principles of the Solvency II Directive should not be questioned in the review (including the confidence level underlying the calibration of capital requirements and the market-consistent valuation) (European Commission 2019b).

The European Commission requested a broad-based review across 19 different areas, which can be broadly divided into three parts:

1. Long-term guarantee measures and measures on equity risk;
2. The introduction of new regulatory tools to Solvency II on macro-prudential issues, recovery and resolution, and insurance guarantee schemes;
3. Revisions to the existing Solvency II framework based on the supervisory experience during the first years of its application, in particular to improve on the proportionate and consistent application of its requirements.

It is a wide-ranging review of Solvency II, in part in areas in which the Directive itself envisages a review by January 2021, in part on issues further identified by the Commission in the afore-mentioned call for advice addressed to the EIOPA. It would be preferable, in any case, the Solvency II review might offer the possibility to also correct some cases of distortion, so as to define a new balance between the protection of policyholders, the sound and prudent management of insurance companies and the rule that the insurance sector must perform in support of economic growth in various countries.

Currently, the European playing field, in terms of insurance regulation and supervision, is not always level. For example, the cross-border operations of European insurance companies are treated differently by the various national supervisory authorities, and this generates different levels of protection for policyholders. Some recent default cases that caused losses to policyholders in various countries would require coordinated interventions. Indeed, a wider harmonisation of national standards per sé, where necessary, is not sufficient: there is also need for greater convergence in supervisory practices.

It is also preferable that some excessively severe legislative constraints, though with the necessary prudence, be mitigated for insurance companies that intend to invest in certain asset classes. Solvency II has already been amended with a view to removing useless obstacles to economic growth, with respect to investment in infrastructure and standardised and transparent securitisation. Further amendments could be introduced for investments in bonds with no rating and unlisted equity securities, with all the necessary precautions.

It is important for insurance companies, as long-term investors, to take account of environmental, social and governance factors in their investments and when creating products, and to provide the public with information about these risks. Nevertheless, from a prudential point of view, it is equally as important that sustainable and green investments be covered by adequate requirements that reflect the specific underlying risks, so that the fair protection of policyholders is not at risk.

The next Solvency II review must therefore ensure not to hinder the harmonious development of the insurance industry, at the same time without losing the capacity to regulate and supervise the system to protect the soundness of the system and individual companies.

References

Albrecher, H., Bommier, A., Filipović, D., Koch-Medina, P., Loisel, S., & Schmeiser, H. (2019). Insurance: Models, Digitalization, and Data Science. *European Actuarial Journal, 9*(2), 349–360.

Bacani, B., McDaniels, J., & Robins, N. (2015). *Insurance 2030: Harnessing Insurance for Sustainable Development* (Inquiry-Psi Working Paper 15/01), 1–37.

Balasubramanian, R., Libarikian, A., & McElhaney, D. (2018, May). *Insurance 2030—The Impact of AI on the Future of Insurance.* Mc Kinsey & Company, Insurance Practice, 1–12.

Baumann, N. (2018). *A Catalyst for Change—How Fintech Has Sparked a Revolution in Insurance.* Available at: https://www2.deloitte.com/content/dam/Deloitte/global/Documents/Financial-Services/gx-fsi-cataylst-for-change.

Behm, S., Deetjen, U., Kaniyar, S., Methner, N., & Münstermann, B. (2019, January). *Digital Ecosystems for Insurers: Opportunities Through the Internet of Things.* McKinsey & Company, Insurance Practice, 1–10.

Billio, M., Getmansky, M., Lo, A., & Pelizzon, A. (2012). Econometric Measures of Connectedness and Systemic Risk in the Finance and Insurance Sectors. *Journal of Financial Economics, 104*(3), 535–559.

Braun, A., & Schreiber, F. (2017). *The Current InsurTech Landscape: Business Models and Disruptive Potential.* St. Gallen: Institute of Insurance Economics I.VW-HSG, University of St. Gallen.

Buehler, K., Carpineti, M., Kerjan, E. M., Nauck, F., & Serino, L. (2019). The Value for Insurers in Better Management of Non Financial Risk. *McKinsey on Risk, 9,* 1–6.

Capgemini and Efma. (2019). *World Insurance Report 2019.* Available at: https://www.efma.com/study/detail/30818.

Cappiello, A. (2018). *Technology and the Insurance Industry: Re-configuring the Competitive Landscape.* Cham: Springer.

Catlin, T., Lorenz, J. T., Nandan, J., Sharma, S., & Waschto, A. (2018, January). *Insurance Beyond Digital: The Rise of Ecosystems and Platforms.* McKinsey & Company, Insurance Practice.

Committee of Sponsoring Organizations (CoSO). (1992). *Internal Control Integrated Framework.*

CRO Forum. (2005). *A Framework for Incorporating Diversification in the Solvency Assessment of Insurers,* 1–52.

CRO Forum. (2015). *Sound Risk Culture in the Insurance Industry,* 1–24.

CRO Forum. (2018). *Understanding and Managing the IT Risk Landscape,* 1–50.

CRO Forum. (2019). *Insurance and Distributed Ledger Technology: A Risk Manager's Perspective Amsterdam,* 1–33.

Deloitte. (2018a, February). *Volatility Adjustment Under the Loop,* 1–26. Available at: https://www2.deloitte.com/content/dam/Deloitte/ch/Documents/financial-services/ch-fs-volatility-adjustment-under-the-loop-final.pdf.

Deloitte. (2018b). *A Catalyst for Change: How Fintech Has Sparked a Revolution in Insurance.* Available at: https://www2.deloitte.com/content/dam/Deloitte/global/Documents/Financial-Services/gx-fsi-cataylst-for-change.pdf.

Egan, R., Cartagena, S., Mohamed, R., Gosrani, V., Grewal, J., Acharyya, M., et al. (2019). Cyber Operational Risk Scenarios for Insurance Companies. *British Actuarial Journal, 24,* e6.

EIOPA. (2017). *Opinion the Supervisory Assessment of Internal Models Including a Dynamic Volatility Adjustment.* Full Press Release. Available at: https://eiopa.europa.eu/Publications/Opinions/2017-12-20%20EIOPA-BoS-17-366_Internal_model_DVA_Opinion.pdf.

EIOPA. (2018a, November). *Sustainable Finance in Insurance and Pensions*. Available at: https://eiopa.europa.eu/Publications/Meetings/05._Joint_BoS_SHG_meeting_Sustainable_Finance.pdf.

EIOPA. (2018b, December). *Report on Long-Term Guarantees Measures and Measures on Equity Risk*.

EIOPA. (2019a). *Cyber Risk for Insurers—Challengers and Opportunities*. Luxembourg: Publications Office of the European Union.

EIOPA (2019b, June). *Solvency II 2020 Review* (EIOPA-IRSG-19/025). Frankfurt, 1–6.

EIOPA. (2019c, September). *Technical Documentation of the Methodology to Derive EIOPA's Risk-Free Interest Rate Term Structures*, 1–133.

EIOPA. (2019d, October). *Consultation Paper on the Opinion on the 2020 review of Solvency II*, 1–739. Available at: https://eiopa.europa.eu/Publications/Consultations/EIOPA-BoS-19-465_CP_Opinion_2020_review.pdf.

Eling, M., & Lehmann, M. (2018). The Impact of Digitalization on the Insurance Value Chain and the Insurability of Risks. *The Geneva Papers, 43*, 359–396.

Ernst & Young (EY). (2017). *GDPR: Demanding New Privacy Rights and Obligations Perspectives for Non-EU Financial Services Firms* (pp. 1–15). London: EYGM Limited.

Estrella, A. (2001). Mixing and Matching: Prospective Financial Sector Mergers and Market Valuation. *Journal of Banking & Finance, 25*(12), 2367–2392.

European Commission. (2019a, June). *Taxonomy Technical Report*. Available at: https://ec.europa.eu/info/sites/info/files/business_economy_euro/banking_and_finance/documents/190618-sustainable-finance-teg-report-taxonomy_en.pdf.

European Commission. (2019b). *Request to EIOPA for Technical Advice on the Solvency II Directive*. Ref. Ares(2019)782244.

Grima, S. (2019). *The Impact of Technology Innovations on the Governance of Insurance Firms: A Literature Review*. 20th AIDA Conference: Insurance Law and Practice—Current Trends. Future Challenges, Palic, Serbia.

Keller, K. (2018, April). *Data Protection Standards Need to be Global, Wired*. Available at: https://www.gamebreakingnews.net/2018/04/data-protection-standards-need-to-be-global/.

Mackenzie, A. (2015). The Fintech Revolution. *London Business School Review, 26*(3), 50–53.

Marullo, R. (2018). *La gestione dei rischi assicurativi e le revisioni future della regolamentazione Solvency II*. Ania, Roma: XII Congresso nazionale degli attuari.

Mendoza, E., & Quadrini, V. (2010). Financial Globalization, Financial Crises and Contagion. *Journal of Monetary Economics, 57*(2010), 24–39.

Naisbitt, J. (1982). *Megatrends: Ten New Directions Transforming Our Lives.* New York, NY: Warner Books.

OECD. (2017a). *Technology and Innovation in the Insurance Sector.* Available at: https://www.oecd.org/pensions/Technology-and-innovation-in-the-insurance-sector.pdf.

OECD. (2017b). *Investment Governance and the Integration of Environmental, Social and Governance Factors.* Available at: https://www.oecd.org/finance/Investment-Governance-Integration-ESG-Factors.pdf.

OECD. (2019). *Global Insurance Market Trends.* Available at: https://www.oecd.org/finance/globalinsurancemarkettrends.htm.

Pwc. (2019, April). *Re-inventing Internal Controls in the Digital Age.* Available at: https://www.pwc.com/sg/en/publications/assets/reinventing-internal-controls-in-the-digital-age-201904.pdf.

Rae, R. A., Barrett, A., Brooks, D., Chotai, M. A., Pelkiewicz, A. J., & Wang, C. (2018). A Review of Solvency II: Has It Met Its Objectives? *British Actuarial Journal, 23*(4), 1–72.

Richard, P. (2016). Amending the Solvency II VA to Promote Good Risk Management. *Insurance ERM.* Available at: https://www.insuranceerm.com/analysis/amending-the-solvency-ii-va-to-promote-good-risk-management.html.

Schmautz, M. (Ed.). (2016). *Modernising Insurance Solvency Regimes—Key Features of Selected Markets.* Zurich: The Geneva Association.

Schmidt, C. (2018). *Insurance in the Digital Age.* Zurich: The Geneva Association.

Slepov, V. A., Kosov, M. E., Chalova, A. Y., Gromova, E. I., & Voronkova, E. K. (2019). Integration of the Financial Market Sectors: Factors, Risks and Management Approaches. *International Journal of Mechanical Engineering and Technology, 10*(2), 1243–1250.

Swiss Re Institute. (2017, June). T*echnology and Insurance: Themes and Challenges.* Available at: https://www.swissre.com/dam/jcr:85c4ccde-50b7-41cf-a2df-d365cc35a6f4/expertise_publication_technology_and_insurance_themes_and_challenges.pdft20150523T033833__w__/sgen/_acnmedia/Accenture/Conversion-Assets/DotCom/Documents/Global/PDF.

The Geneva Association. (2018). *Climate Change and the Insurance Industry: Taking Action as Risk Managers and Investors.* Available at: https://www.genevaassociation.org/sites/default/files/research-topics-document-type/pdf_public/climate_change_and_the_insurance_industry_-_taking_action_as_risk_managers_and_investors.pdf.

United Nations Environment Programme (UNEP). (2009). *The Global State of Sustainable Insurance.* Understanding and Integrating Environmental, Social and Governance Factors in Insurance. Available at: https://www.unepfi.org/fileadmin/documents/global-state-of-sustainable-insurance_01.pdf.

United Nations Environment Programme (UNEP). (2019). *Underwriting Environmental, Social and Governance Risks in Non-life Insurance Business*, 1–38.

Vanderlinden, S. L., Millie, S. M., Anderson, N., & Chishti, S. (2018). *The InsurTech Book: The Insurance Technology Handbook for Investors, Entrepreneurs and FinTech Visionaries*. Hoboken: Wiley.

Voutilainen, R., & Koskinen, L. (2019). Megatrends in the Insurance. In A. Kangas. J. Kujala, A. Heikkinen, A. Lonnqvist, H. Laihonen, & J. Bethwaite (Eds.), *Leading Change in a Complex World: Transdisciplinary Perspectives and Financial Sector*. Tampere, Finland: Tampere University Press.

World Economic Forum (WEF). (2018). *The Global Risks Report 2018* (13th ed.). Geneva.

CHAPTER 6

An Assessment Model of the Internal Controls System

Abstract The chapter focuses on the internal audit function—the third line of defence within the internal control system—whose main purpose is to verify the operational efficacy and efficiency of internal controls. In this regard, an assessment model is proposed, in order to enable the Internal Audit function to express a synthetic opinion of the company's internal control system on an annual basis. The model is constructed starting from the risk types defined by the company organisational model, identified within the entity-level risks (which affect the overall company structure) and within the process-level risks, which affect individual company processes and are influenced by the former.

Keywords Internal audit function · Risk governance · Risk assessment · Internal controls system · Inherent risk · Residual risk

1 Introduction

In the last decade, the financial crisis that put a substantial amount of insurance undertakings and groups under severe financial distress brought the attention of insurers and supervisory authorities to the strategic importance of good governance practices in order to guarantee sound

A. Cappiello, *The European Insurance Industry*,
https://doi.org/10.1007/978-3-030-43142-6_6

and prudent management. Indeed, among other reasons, the distress was attributable to inappropriate investment decisions by insurers which led to significant losses, interconnectedness with banks and, in general, evidence of poor governance (Boubakri 2011; Dell'Atti and Sylos Labini 2019).

In this respect, the results that emerged from the Sharma Report (European Commission 2002) are illuminating, in that they provided useful insight into the dynamics of insurance failures. The report concluded that there is usually a causal chain of multiple causes, starting with underlying internal problems in the insurer (usually coupled with poor management) that eventually lead to inadequate decision-making and neglectful risk decisions. This makes those firms vulnerable to external "trigger events", which in turn will lead to adverse financial outcomes, as well as policyholders' losses in some cases.

To help supervisors and policymakers understand the leading causes of failure and near misses (near failures) in insurance, in 2018 the European Insurance and Occupational Pensions Authority (EIOPA) published a report based on the information contained in the EIOPA database, which comprises a sample of 180 affected insurance undertakings in 31 European countries, dating from 1999 to 2016 (EIOPA 2018).

An overall analysis of the causes of failure and near misses for the EU insurers in the database, as identified by supervisors, reveals a multiplicity of impairment factors that do not differ greatly from the findings published in the Sharma Report.

The analysis states that the two most common general causes of failures and near misses identified for the EU insurers in the database are linked to underlying internal company risks, namely: (i) the risk that management or staff lack the necessary skills, experience or professional qualities (management and staff competence risk); and (ii) the risk of inadequate or failed systems of corporate governance and overall control (internal governance and control risk).

2 The Internal Audit Assessment of the Internal Controls System

A sound internal controls system cannot disregard an effective and comprehensive internal audit function—the third line of defence also ensued by the Solvency II risk governance framework—in keeping with the diversity and complexity of the insurance undertaking's activity (see Chapter 4) (Ernst & Young 2018).

Among other duties and responsibilities, the internal audit function assesses whether the significant risks of the organisation are appropriately identified and reported by management to the supervisory body, whether those risks are appropriately mitigated and whether the organisation operates in an efficient and effective manner (IIA 2009, 2013; D'Onza 2013; ECIIA 2019).

The model we show is implemented in order to allow the internal audit function to present to the Board an annual synthetic assessment of the company's internal controls system. The model is constructed taking into account the risk types defined by the company's organisational model, namely:

1. Entity-level risks, which impact the overall system of the company;
2. process-level risks, linked to the operations of the company, which impact the individual company processes. These are influenced by the first type of risk.

Depending on the type of risk, the company provides specific: (i) entity-level controls and (ii) process-level controls.

By rating the identified risk factors, the model obtains, through a system of weighting and reaggregation, a synthetic assessment of the overall control system, assuming that the residual risks at the entity level affect the 30% of internal controls system, while the company process influence the remaining 70%.

The assessment of the overall internal controls system is expressed as a numerical scale from 1 to 5, which relates back to a synthetic residual risk rating based on Table 17 in the Appendix.

The development of the internal audit assessment process is shown in detail below.

3 The Assessment of Entity-Level Residual Risk

The assessment process of the overall residual risk at entity level is calculated through the weighting of the residual risk values assigned to each of the 25 identified risk factors, as shown in Table 10 in the Appendix.

The weighting is firstly performed within each component of the internal controls system (control culture; risk control and assessment; control activities; information and communication; monitoring), subsequently between the ratings of the various components.

Table 1 Rating conversion table

Qualitative rating	*Numerical rating*
Favourable	1
Prevalently favourable	2
Partially favourable	3
Prevalently unfavourable	4
Unfavourable	5

The residual risk of each risk factor, since these are elements that impact the overall company's governance, is not calculated as a direct combination of the inherent risk with the controls designated to mitigate it, but through a methodology that takes implicit account of the elements that form the risk factor. Therefore, for each risk factor, the internal audit function: (i) identifies the parameters that allow for the assessment of the risk factor; (ii) for each parameter, it expresses a qualitative rating that takes implicit account of the inherent risk and related controls. Each qualitative rating corresponds to a numerical rating expressed on a scale from 1 to 5 (see Table 1).

The residual risk of each risk factor is given by the arithmetic average of the numerical ratings assigned to each of the parameters.

Tables 2, 3, 4, 5, and 6 show the ratings of residual risks of the 25 risk factors that impact the internal controls system at the entity level (for details of the method of calculating see Tables from 12 to 17 in the Appendix).

After calculating the ratings of the residual risks of the 25 risk factors, the assessment of the overall residual risk at the entity level, deriving from the weighting ad aggregation of the ratings of these risk factors—based on Table 17 in the Appendix—receives a qualitative rating of "R2 – Low", on the basis of the numerical value of 2.09, as shown in the following Table 7.

4 The Assessment of Process-Level Residual Risk

The evaluation of the overall residual risk of the operating processes is calculated by weighting the residual risks assigned to the individual processes audited during the period of observation.

Firstly, internal audit identifies the risks (and for each one the correlated risk factors) impacting the various phases that form the processes under analysis. The risk identification is achieved with support from

Table 2 Control environment residual risks

Risk factor	Evaluation parameters	Summary description	Qualitative rating	Rating	Residual risk
1 – Ethical Code	Is the company's ethical code updated in terms of internal/external legislation?	Yes	FAVOURABLE	1	
	Have disciplinary sanctions been imposed on employees during the year?	No	FAVOURABLE	1	
	During the year, were there behaviours in violation of the ethical code by employees?	No	FAVOURABLE	1	
	During the year, were there behaviours in violation of the ethical code by the corporate bodies or members thereof?	No	FAVOURABLE	1	
	EVALUATION FACTOR 1			1.00	R1 - Negligible
2 - Compliance of decisions with enterprise's risk appetite	Were there cases of non-compliance with the enterprise's of risk appetite? If yes, was a report sent to the BoD?	No	FAVOURABLE	1	
	EVALUATION FACTOR 2			1.00	R1 - Negligible
3 - Adequacy of the organisational structure	During the year were there inadequate structure situations?	Need to strengthen the risk management structure	PREVALENTLY UNFAVOURABLE	4	
	Were there operating losses caused by structural shortcomings?	None significant	PREVALENTLY FAVOURABLE	2	
	EVALUATION FACTOR 3			3.00	R3 - Medium
4 - System of powers and proxies	Were there cases of non-compliance with the system of powers and proxies?	Only marginal cases	PREVALENTLY FAVOURABLE	2	
	Is the system of powers and proxies compliant with the legislation of reference?	Yes	FAVOURABLE	1	
	EVALUATION FACTOR 4			1.50	R2 - Low
5 - Budget process	Is there a budget process?	Yes	FAVOURABLE	1	
	Is the budget consistent with the company's risk appetite?	Yes	FAVOURABLE	1	
	Were the operational decisions of senior management consistent with the budget?	Yes, there are only marginal deviations	PREVALENTLY FAVOURABLE	2	
	EVALUATION FACTOR 5			1.33	R1 - Negligible
6 - Remuneration policies	They comply with regulations	Yes	FAVOURABLE	1	
	Were they applied correctly?	The following critical situations are noted: - objectives to be communicated to employees involved with faster time frames; - economic criterion present in the compliance function's objectives.	PARTIALLY FAVOURABLE	3	
	EVALUATION FACTOR 6			2.00	R2 - Low
7 - Training of the distribution network and personnel	Was training performed correctly?	No anti-money laundering training was performed	PREVALENTLY UNFAVOURABLE	4	
	Was training to uphold the certification performed correctly?	Yes	FAVOURABLE	1	
	Are there training plans for company personnel?	It is necessary to reinforce training for the control functions	PARTIALLY FAVOURABLE	3	
	EVALUATION FACTOR 7			2.67	R3 - Medium

the periodic evaluations performed by the risk management, compliance and anti-money laundering/anti-terrorism functions, and from the self-assessments performed by the process owners.

Internal audit assigns to each risk factor its inherent risk rating, deriving from the valuation of the probability of occurrence and impact of the risk event (see Tables 12 and 13 in the Appendix).

On the basis of evaluation of the existing controls, the weighted residual risk is calculated for each process phase analysed during the audits.

Table 3 Risk assessment activities residual risks

Risk factor	Evaluation parameters	Summary description	Qualitative rating	Rating	Residual risk
8 - Correct risk mapping	Were all the risks identified?	Only marginal risks are missing	PREVALENTLY FAVOURABLE	2	
	Is the risk mapping carried out each year?	No, the last version dates from the previous year	PARTIALLY FAVOURABLE	3	
	Is there a full list of the risks to which the company is exposed?	Present but incomplete and not updated	PREVALENTLY UNFAVOURABLE	4	
	EVALUATION FACTOR 8			**3.00**	**R3 - Medium**
9 - Event identification and risk measurement	Is there a risk self-assessment by the process owners?	Only for the IT area and administration and finance area processes	PREVALENTLY UNFAVOURABLE	4	
	Is the risk assessment/self-assessment carried out each year?	No, there are cases of self-assessments not updated for 2 years	PREVALENTLY UNFAVOURABLE	4	
	Were the risks assessed correctly?	Yes, there are marginal aspects to be improved	PARTIALLY FAVOURABLE	3	
	EVALUATION FACTOR 9			**3.67**	**R4 - High**
10 - Risk mitigation	Were controls provided for each risk identified?	Yes, even if there are controls to be made more efficient	PARTIALLY FAVOURABLE	3	
	Was a manager identified for each control?	Yes	FAVOURABLE	1	
	EVALUATION FACTOR 10			**2.00**	**R2 - Low**
11 - Adequacy and efficiency of the level 2 control functions	Adequacy and efficiency of the Risk Management function	Some delays found	PARTIALLY FAVOURABLE	3	
	Adequacy and efficiency of the Compliance function	It is necessary to guarantee better time frames in the preparation of the gap analyses	PARTIALLY FAVOURABLE	3	
	Adequacy and efficiency of the Anti-Money Laundering and Anti-Terrorism function	It is necessary to improve reporting to the corporate bodies involved (BoD, BoA, etc.)	PREVALENTLY FAVOURABLE	2	
	Adequacy and efficiency of the Actuarial function	Improvements and efficiency measures on marginal aspects	PREVALENTLY FAVOURABLE	2	
	EVALUATION FACTOR 11			**2.50**	**R3 - Medium**

The residual risk of the process is then obtained as the weighted sum of the residual risks of the individual process phases.

Once the residual risk is calculated for each individual process, the overall residual risk of the company processes is calculated. In particular, internal audit assigns to each process a weighting as a percentage of the overall processes owned by operating area, up to 100%; subsequently, it assigns to the operating area a weighting as a percentage of the overall organisation of the company, up to 100%.

The following steps are then taken:

- calculation of the residual risk value of the individual operating areas: for each operating area the weighted residual risks of the individual processes analysed during the audits are added together. The weighting factor of each audited process is calculated as the percentage of the process on the total processes owned by the area, re-proportioned between the individual weightings of the processes audited until a figure out of 100 is obtained;

Table 4 Control activities residual risks

Risk factor	Evaluation parameters	Summary description	Qualitative rating	Rating	Residual risk
12 - Accounting and balance sheet	Are there balancing and reconciliation controls (e.g. bank c/a)?	Yes, there are only marginal aspects to be improved	PREVALENTLY FAVOURABLE	2	
	Are there adequate automatic controls of the accounting procedure?	Yes	FAVOURABLE	1	
	EVALUATION FACTOR 12			1.50	R1 - Negligible
13 - Authorisation limits	Are there adequate authorisation limits?	Yes	FAVOURABLE	1	
	Are they respected correctly?	Yes	FAVOURABLE	1	
	EVALUATION FACTOR 13			1.00	R1 - Negligible
14 - Efficiency and adequacy of the fraud prevention system	Are there anti-fraud controls?	There are significant margins for improvement in the definition of a fraud prevention system	PREVALENTLY UNFAVOURABLE	4	
	Are the anti-fraud controls effective?	The current controls are effective	FAVOURABLE	1	
	EVALUATION FACTOR 14			2.50	R3 - Medium
15 - Operating procedures, manuals and instructions	Are they formalised?	Formalisation of non-core processes is missing	PARTIALLY FAVOURABLE	3	
	Are they distributed to company personnel?	Yes	FAVOURABLE	1	
	Is there correspondence between operations and the operating procedures, manuals and instructions?	There are margins for improvement	PARTIALLY FAVOURABLE	3	
	EVALUATION FACTOR 15			2.33	R2 - Low
16 – Segregation of duties	Is there a correct segregation of the tasks between those who perform the operations and those who control them?	Since the firm only employs around twenty individuals, there are marginal cases of failure to separate tasks	PARTIALLY FAVOURABLE	3	
	Is there segregation of functions between those that develop software (new and changes to existing) and those that implement it?	Yes	FAVOURABLE	1	
	EVALUATION FACTOR 16			2.00	R2 - Low
17 - Line controls	Are they designed and implemented correctly?	Yes, there are only marginal aspects to be improved	PREVALENTLY FAVOURABLE	2	
	Are they performed effectively and correctly?	Yes, there are only marginal aspects to be improved	PREVALENTLY FAVOURABLE	2	
	Are they adequately formalised?	Yes, there are only marginal aspects to be improved	PREVALENTLY FAVOURABLE	2	
	EVALUATION FACTOR 17			2.00	R2 - Low
18 - Outsourcing	Is the outsourcing consistent with the specific policies defined by the BoD?	Yes	FAVOURABLE	1	
	Are there adequate Service Levels (SLs) and penalties consistent with them?	It is necessary to guarantee a better correlation between the non-compliance of the SLs by the outsourcer and the penalties to be paid to the company	PREVALENTLY UNFAVOURABLE	4	
	Are there effective controls on the outsourcing activities?	The function in charge of controlling outsourced activities must perform controls entering further into the risks related to the outsourcing activities	PREVALENTLY UNFAVOURABLE	4	
	EVALUATION FACTOR 18			3.00	R3 - Medium

- calculation of the overall residual risk value at process level: the residual risk values of the individual areas involved in the audit are added together on the basis of the weighting of those areas. The weighting factor of each audited area is calculated as the percentage of the individual area on the total areas, re-proportioned between the weightings of the individual areas audited until a figure out of 100 is obtained.

Table 5 Information and communication residual risks

INFORMATION FLOWS					
Risk factor	**Evaluation parameters**	**Summary description**	**Qualitative rating**	**Rating**	**Residual risk**
19 - IT systems (adequacy of infrastructure)	Were there operational losses due to the inadequacy of the IT infrastructure?	Yes, only insignificant losses. Overall the infrastructure is substantially adequate.	PREVALENTLY FAVOURABLE	2	
	EVALUATION FACTOR 19			**2.00**	**R2 - Low**
20 - IT systems (adequacy of support for internal users)	Was a risk-based approach adopted when testing the End User Computing Reports (EUCR)?	No	PREVALENTLY UNFAVOURABLE	4	
	Are the EUCR reliable?	Overall yes. It is necessary however to prepare a survey and periodic monitoring of the EUCR	PREVALENTLY FAVOURABLE	2	
	Are there specific controls of the IT environment (PCs) where the EUCR is used and managed?	No	PREVALENTLY UNFAVOURABLE	4	
	EVALUATION FACTOR 20			**3.33**	**R3 - Medium**
21 - Business Contingency Plan	Is there a Business Contingency Plan?	Yes	FAVOURABLE	1	
	Are Disaster & Recovery and Continuity tests performed annually?	Yes	FAVOURABLE	1	
	EVALUATION FACTOR 21			**1.00**	**R1 - Negligible**
22 - Information security	Are there programmes that guarantee adequate data quality standards?	Yes, there are aspects for improvement	PREVALENTLY FAVOURABLE	2	
	Adequacy of procedures to access programmes and data	Two cases of staff in the distribution network authorised to sell policies in absence of insurance certification	PREVALENTLY UNFAVOURABLE	4	
	Adequacy of procedures to change programmes	It is necessary to formalise these more adequately	PARTIALLY FAVOURABLE	3	
	Adequacy of the procedures to develop the systems	Adequate procedures	FAVOURABLE	1	
	Adequacy of the IT services	Adequate procedures	FAVOURABLE	1	
	EVALUATION FACTOR 22			**2.00**	**R2 - Low**
23 - Reporting flows between the Board plus other control bodies and the operational line	Are there effective periodic reporting flows?	Yes, it is necessary however to prepare periodic flows to the SB 231/01 (in particular regarding exceptions to policy contracts)	PREVALENTLY FAVOURABLE	2	
	Are there corrective mechanisms in the event that anomalies are found?	Yes, it is necessary to formalise and regulate them	PREVALENTLY FAVOURABLE	2	
	EVALUATION FACTOR 23			**2.00**	**R2 - Low**

Table 6 Monitoring residual risks

Risk factor	**Evaluation parameters**	**Summary description**	**Qualitative rating**	**Rati ng**	**Residual risk**
24 - Follow-up of corrective actions	Are critical situations encountered resolved promptly at all levels?	Yes, it is necessary however to guarantee better time frames in resolving less risky critical situations	PREVALENTLY FAVOURABLE	2	
	Is there a definitive removal of the causes of the critical situations encountered at all levels?	Yes, it is necessary however to guarantee better time frames in resolving less risky critical situations	PREVALENTLY FAVOURABLE	2	
	Are the action plans to resolve the audit findings respected?	Yes, even if there is re-planning of the resolution time frames	PARTIALLY FAVOURABLE	3	
	EVALUATION FACTOR 24			**2.33**	**R2 - Low**
25 - Efficiency of the internal auditing	Was the audit plan completed?	Completed	FAVOURABLE	1	
	EVALUATION FACTOR 25			**1.00**	**R1 - Negligible**

Table 7 Residual risk assessment at entity level

ICS components	Factor no.	Risk factor	Residual risk	Risk value	Factor weighting	Evaluation of components	Components weighting	Overall entity level evaluation
Control Environment	1	Ethical Code	R1 – Negligible	1.00	10%	0.10		
	2	Compliance of decisions with enterprise's risk appetite	R1 – Negligible	1.00	20%	0.20		
	3	Adequacy of the organisational structure in terms of risks	R3 – Medium	3.00	15%	0.45		
	4	System of powers and proxies	R2 – Low	1.50	20%	0.30		
	5	Budget process	R1 – Negligible	1.33	10%	0.13		
	6	Remuneration policies	R2 – Low	2.00	15%	0.30		
	7	Training of the distribution network and personnel	R3 – Medium	2.67	10%	0.27		
	WEIGHTED "CONTROL ENVIRONMENT"				100%	1.75	25%	0.44
Risk and Control Assessment	8	Correct risk mapping	R3 – Medium	3.00	25%	0.75		
	9	Event identification and risk measurement	R4 – High	3.67	30%	1.10		
	10	Risk mitigation	R2 – Low	2.00	25%	0.50		
	11	Adequacy and efficiency of the level 2 control functions	R3 – Medium	2.50	20%	0.50		
	WEIGHTED "RISK AND CONTROL ASSESSMENT"				100%	2.85	20%	0.57
Control Activities	12	Accounting and balance sheet	R1 – Negligible	1.50	10%	0.15		
	13	Authorisation limits	R1 – Negligible	1.00	15%	0.15		
	14	Efficiency and adequacy of the fraud prevention system	R3 – Medium	2.50	5%	0.13		
	15	Operating procedures, manuals and instructions	R2 – Low	2.33	10%	0.23		
	16	Segregation of duties	R2 – Low	2.00	20%	0.40		
	17	Line controls	R2 – Low	2.00	20%	0.40		
	18	Outsourcing	R3 – Medium	3.00	20%	0.60		
	WEIGHTED "CONTROL ACTIVITIES"				100%	2.06	20%	0.41
Information and Communication	19	IT systems (adequacy of infrastructure)	R2 – Low	2.00	20%	0.40		
	20	IT systems (adequacy of support for internal users)	R3 – Medium	3.33	15%	0.50		
	21	Business Contingency Plan	R1 – Negligible	1.00	20%	0.20		
	22	Information security	R2 – Low	2.00	20%	0.40		
	23	Reporting flows between the Board plus other control bodies and the operational line	R2 – Low	2.00	25%	0.50		
	WEIGHTED "INFORMATION FLOWS"				100%	2.00	20%	0.40
Monitoring	24	Follow-up of corrective actions	R2 – Low	2.33	60%	1.40		
	25	Efficiency of the internal auditing	R1 – Negligible	1	40%	0.40		
	WEIGHTED "MONITORING"				100%	1.80	15%	0.27
OVERALL ASSESSMENT OF THE "ENTITY LEVEL" RISKS AND CONTROLS			R2 – Low				100%	2.09

The overall process of assessment is carried out on the basis of the criteria shown in the Tables from 12 to 17 in the Appendix.

Table 8 shows the calculation of the overall residual risk of the operating processes, taking into account that during the period at issue, internal audit performed the following activities envisaged in the audit plan:

Table 8 Residual risk assessment at process level

		PROCESS			AREA			COMPANY (process level)			
Area	Company process	Process weighting	Process audited	Residual risk	Process weighting factor		Residual risk	Area weighting	Area weighting factor		Residual risk
Administration and finance	Taxation management	10%	NO		0%	0.00	0.00				
	Cash management	5%	NO		0%	0.00	0.00				
	Commissions management	5%	NO		0%	0.00	0.00				
	Collection and bookkeeping of premiums	10%	NO		0%	0.00	0.00				
	Financial statement drafting process	20%	NO		0%	0.00	0.00				
	Finance and securities trading	20%	NO		0%	0.00	0.00				
	Expenses reimbursement	5%	YES	1.80	5%	0.25	0.45				
	Management of suppliers	5%	NO		0%	0.00	0.00				
	Payments	15%	YES	2.8	15%	0.75	2.10				
	Financial management of pension products	5%	NO		0%	0.00	0.00				
	EVALUATION	*100%*			*20%*	*1.00*	*2.55*	*20%*	*20%*	*0.20*	*0.51*
Portfolio management	Management of Index Linked products	20%	NO		0%	0.00	0.00				
	Management of Life products	30%	YES	2.6	30%	0.50	1.30				
	Management of Non-Life products	10%	NO		0%	0.00	0.00				
	Management of Unit Linked products	30%	YES	1.62	30%	0.50	0.81				
	Dormant policies	10%	NO		0%	0.00	0.00				
	EVALUATION	*100%*			*60%*	*1.00*	*2.11*	*25%*	*25%*	*0.25*	*0.53*
Technical – Actuarial	Coinsurance	20%	NO		0%	0	0.00				
	Reinsurance	30%	YES	2.4	30%	1	2.40				
	Management of life and non-life reservation process	35%	NO		0%	0	0.00				
	Development of new products	15%	NO		0%	0	0.00				
	EVALUATION	*100%*			*30%*	*1.00*	*2.40*	*25%*	*25%*	*0.25*	*0.60*
Organisation and complaints	Written complaints	20%	YES	1.28	20%	0.33	0.43				
	Definition and approval of processes	40%	NO		0%	0.00	0.00				
	Training of intermediaries	40%	YES	2.2	40%	0.67	1.47				
	EVALUATION	*100%*			*60%*	*1.00*	*1.89*	*10%*	*10%*	*0.10*	*0.19*
IT	Update to IT procedures	30%	NO		0%	0	0.00				
	Business Contingency Plan process	40%	NO		0%	0	0.00				
	Access to IT systems	30%	YES	3.3	30%	1	3.30				
	EVALUATION	*100%*			*30%*	*1.00*	*3.30*	*20%*	*20%*	*0.20*	*0.66*
OVERALL ASSESSMENT OF THE "PROCESS LEVEL" RISKS AND CONTROLS								100%	100%	1.00	2.49

- audit of the expenses reimbursement process;
- audit of the payment process;
- audit of unit linked products process;
- audit of the issue process of re-evaluable policies;
- audit of the reinsurance process;
- audit of the process to access IT systems by management team users;
- audit of written complaints process; and
- audit of intermediaries training process.

5 Conclusions

As recalled above, the overall rating of the internal control system is expressed as a weighting of the values of the residual risk at entity and process level. Specifically, it is assumed that the risks at entity level impact on the 30% of the internal control system, while the remaining 70% is influenced by the operating activities (process level).

In the event of evaluating the company's internal control system, the analysis shows an overall residual risk of "R2 – Low", equal to 2.37, given by the weighting of the residual risk "R2 – Low" at entity level and the residual risk "R3 – Medium" of the company processes (for details of the method of calculating see Tables from 12 to 17 in the Appendix).

The table to evaluate the residual risk of the company's internal controls system is shown in Table 9.

The rating of the internal control system reported to the Board with the internal audit report substantially proves positive. The overall residual risk has a low impact and may be considered acceptable.

Nevertheless, it is necessary to guarantee a policy to maintain the situation reported through periodic monitoring by the senior management and by management, and also to act to remove the main risks reported at entity and process level. In this regard, the risk factors—at both entity and process level—with a residual risk of "R4 – High" and/or "R5 – Very high" and the main factors that have a residual risk of "R3 – Medium", must be highlighted to ensure that the Board and senior management implement the necessary containment and mitigation actions for the risks shown.

Table 9 Final assessment of the overall residual risk

	Residual risk	Value	Factor weighting	Factor evaluation
ENTITY LEVEL	R2 – Low	2.09	30%	0.63
PROCESS LEVEL	R3 – Medium	2.49	70%	1.74
COMPANY	R2 – Low		**100%**	2.37

Appendix

See Tables 10, 11, 12, 13, 14, 15, 16, and 17.

Table 10 Entity level risk factors

ICS components	*Factor No.*	*Risk factor*
Control environment	1	Ethical code
	2	Compliance of decisions with enterprise's risk appetite
	3	Adequacy of the organisational structure in terms of risks
	4	System of powers and proxies
	5	Budget process
	6	Remuneration policies
	7	Training of the distribution network and personnel
Risk assessment	8	Correct risk mapping
	9	Event identification and risk measurement
	10	Risk mitigation
	11	Adequacy and efficiency of the level 2 control functions
Control activities	12	Accounting and balance sheet
	13	Authorisation limits
	14	Efficiency and adequacy of the fraud prevention system
	15	Operating procedures, manuals and instructions
	16	Segregation of duties
	17	Line controls
	18	Outsourcing
Information and communication	19	IT systems (adequacy of infrastructure)
	20	IT systems (adequacy of support for internal users)
	21	Business Contingency Plan
	22	Information security
	23	Reporting flows between the Board plus other control bodies and the operational line
Monitoring	24	Follow-up of corrective actions
	25	Efficiency of the internal auditing

Table 11 Process level risk factors

		Risks								
Area	*Company process*	*Underwriting*	*Reserving*	*Market*	*Credit*	*Liquidity*	*Operational*	*Compliance*	*Reputational*	*Money laundering and terrorism*
Administration and finance	Taxation management						X	X	X	X
	Cash management						X	X	X	X
	Commissions management						X	X	X	
	Collection and bookkeeping of premiums						X	X	X	X
	Financial statement drafting process						X	X	X	
	Finance and securities trading	X	X	X	X	X	X	X	X	
	Expenses reimbursement						X	X	X	
	Management of suppliers						X	X	X	
	Payments						X	X	X	X
	Financial management of pension products			X	X	X	X	X	X	

(continued)

Table 11 (continued)

		Risks								
Area	*Company process*	*Underwriting*	*Reserving*	*Market*	*Credit*	*Liquidity*	*Operational*	*Compliance*	*Reputational*	*Money laundering and terrorism*
Portfolio management	Management of index-linked products	X					X	X	X	X
	Management of life products	X					X	X	X	X
	Management of non-life products	X					X	X	X	
	Management of unit-linked products	X					X	X	X	X
	Dormant policies						X	X	X	
Technical—Actuarial	Coinsurance	X			X		X	X	X	
	Reinsurance	X			X		X	X	X	
	Management of life and non-life reservation process	X	X				X	X	X	
	Development of new products	X					X	X	X	

		Risks								
Area	*Company process*	*Underwriting*	*Reserving*	*Market*	*Credit*	*Liquidity*	*Operational*	*Compliance*	*Reputational*	*Money laundering and terrorism*
Organisation and complaints	Written complaints						X	X	X	
	Definition and approval of processes						X			
	Training of intermediaries						X	X	X	
IT	Update to IT procedures						X	X	X	
	Business contingency plan process						X	X	X	
	Access to IT systems						X	X	X	

Table 12 Probability of occurrence

Rating	*Description*
Low	The risk event occurs with a low frequency as regards the operations affected
Medium	The risk event occurs with a medium frequency as regards the operations affected
High	The risk event occurs with a high frequency. Typical type of processes that involve standardised and repetitive operations

Table 13 Impact of the risk event

RATING	Economic	Executive	Reputational
R1 - Negligible	Negligible capital or income impact, no worsening of performance.	The abnormal event causes extraordinary delays, reworks and recoveries absorbed by ordinary management.	No media coverage; occasional customer complaints.
R2 - Low	Slight capital or income impact; slight worsening of performance.	The abnormal event causes extraordinary delays, reworks and recoveries absorbed by specific planning. Additions to processes and controls may be necessary. Complete compliance with legislation or physical/information security is not guaranteed.	Possible local media coverage and/or limited increase of customer complaints.
R3 - Medium	Perceptible capital or income impact; perceptible worsening of performance.	The abnormal event causes significant extraordinary delays, reworks and recoveries with the need to review the work processes and/or controls. Compliance with legislation or physical/information security is not guaranteed.	Local media coverage and/or considerable increase of complaints with loss of customers.
R4 - High	Capital or income impact leading to a worsening of company performance.	The resolution of the abnormal event requires prompt intervention to reorganise the work processes audited and/or the controls. The abnormal event seriously compromises the compliance with the internal and external legislation and physical and information security.	National media coverage and/or high loss of customers. Reputation risk in terms of the Supervisory Authority.
R5 - Very High	Possible compromise of the companyís capital soundness before generating consequences for its business continuity.	The resolution of the abnormal event requires immediate intervention to radically change the structure leading to an overall reorganisation of the work processes, monitoring controls and the infrastructure used.	High national media coverage and/or worrying loss of customers. High reputation risk in terms of the Supervisory Authority.

Table 14 Evaluation matrix of the inherent risk

		PROBABILITY OF OCCURRENCE		
		Low	**Medium**	**High**
IMPACT OF THE RISK EVENT	**Negligible**	Negligible (R1)	Negligible (R1)	Low (R2)
	Low	Negligible (R1)	Low (R2)	Medium (R3)
	Medium	Low (R2)	Medium (R3)	High (R4)
	High	Medium (R3)	High (R4)	Very High (R5)
	Very High	High (R4)	Very High (R5)	Very High (R5)

Table 15 Controls rating

Rating	*Description*
Absent	Control non-existent
Ineffective	Inadequate control characterised by weaknesses and shortcomings that do not make it possible to mitigate the risk
Satisfactory	Control that presents areas for improvement in order to mitigate the risk effectively and systematically
Effective	Control that mitigates the risk effectively and systematically

Table 16 Evaluation scale of the residual risk

RESIDUAL RISK	Description	Average range of the numerical ratings	
		Min.	Max.
R1 - Negligible	Acceptable residual risk. It is necessary to implement a ìmaintenance policyî through periodic monitoring by the management team involved.	0	1.4
R2 - Low	Low-impact residual risk, deemed nevertheless acceptable. It is necessary to implement a ìmaintenance policyî through periodic monitoring by the management team involved.	1.4	2.4
R3 - Medium	Medium-impact residual risk and/or with low probability of occurrence. The management team of reference must be directly involved in the mitigation actions.	2.4	3.4
R4 - High	High-impact residual risk and/or with high probability of occurrence. High involvement of the management team of reference in the mitigation and monitoring actions by Senior Management.	3.4	4.4
R5 - Very high	Very high-impact residual risk for the company and/or with very high probability of occurrence. Senior Management must be directly involved in the mitigation actions and there must be direct monitoring by the Board of Directors.	4.4	5

Table 17 Evaluation matrix of the residual risk

		POTENTIAL RISK				
		Negligible	*Low*	*Medium*	*High*	*Very High*
CONTROLS	*Absent*	Negligible (R1)	Low (R2)	Medium (R3)	High (R4)	Very High (R5)
	Ineffective	Negligible (R1)	Low (R2)	Medium (R3)	High (R4)	Very High (R5)
	Satisfactory	Negligible (R1)	Negligible (R1)	Low (R2)	Medium (R3)	High (R4)
	Effective	Negligible (R1)	Negligible (R1)	Negligible (R1)	Negligible (R1)	Negligible (R1)

References

Boubakri, N. (2011). Corporate Governance and Issues from the Insurance Industry. *Journal of Risk and Insurance, 78*(3), 501.

Dell'Atti, S., & Sylos Labini, S. (2019). *Il governo societario nelle imprese di assicurazione*. Regolamentazione, proporzionalità e gestione del cambiamento. Wolters Kluwer, Milano.

D'Onza, G. (2013). *L'internal auditing. Profili organizzativi, dinamica di funzionamento e creazine del valore*. Torino: Giappichelli.

ECIIA Insurance Committee. (2019, June). *Internal Audit in the Insurance Industry Guidance*.

EIOPA—European Insurance and Occupational Pensions Authority. (2018). *Failures and Near Misses in Insurance*, pp. 1–52. Luxembourg.

Ernst & Young. (2018). *Internal Audit in Insurance—Current Market Issues and Trends*. Available at: https://www.ey.com/Publication/vwLUAssets/EY-internal-audit-in-insurance/$FILE/EY-internal-audit-in-insurance.pdf.

European Commission. (2002, December). *Report on the Prudential Supervision of Insurance Undertakings* (Sharma Report). Conference of Insurance Supervisory Services of the Member States of the European Union.

IIA—The Institute of Internal Auditors. (2009). *The Role of Internal Auditing in Enterprise-Wide Risk Management*. Altamonte Springs, FL: IIA Inc.

IIA—Institute of Internal Auditors. (2013). *Guidance on Effective Internal Audit in the Financial Service Sector*. Available at: https://www.iia.org.uk/resources/sector-specific-standards-guidance/financial-services/financial-services-code/.

Index

A. Cappiello, *The European Insurance Industry*,
https://doi.org/10.1007/978-3-030-43142-6

The manufacturer's authorised representative in the EU is Springer Nature Customer Service Centre GmbH, Europaplatz 3, 69115 Heidelberg, Germany. If you have any concerns regarding our products, please contact ProductSafety@springernature.com

Printed and bound by CPI Group (UK) Ltd, Croydon, CR0 4YY
30/09/2026
02225609-0005